ITALIAN RENAISSANCE SCULPTURE

ITALIAN RENAISSANCE SCULPTURE

By Andrew Butterfield

WITH ESSAYS BY

Francesco Caglioti

Giancarlo Gentilini

Gert Kreytenberg

Jeanette Sisk

SALANDER-O'REILLY
NEW YORK

This catalogue accompanies an exhibition
from November 3, 2004 to January 8, 2005 at

Salander-O'Reilly Galleries, LLC
20 East 79 Street New York, NY 10021
Tel (212) 879-6606 Fax (212) 744-0655
www.salander.com
Monday–Saturday 9:30 to 5:30

CONTENTS

6 **Master of the Magi of Fabriano**
Madonna and Child

14 **Bartolomeo Bon**
Hope and *Charity*

22 **Urbano da Cortona**
Dead Christ Supported by Two Angels

30 **Giovanni Antonio Amadeo**
Pietà

38 **Benedetto da Maiano**
Head of a Man (Giovanni Serristori?)

48 **Girolamo Santacroce**
Saint John the Baptist and *Saint Benedict*

64 **Maffeo Olivieri**
Candelabrum

74 **Ferdinando Tacca**
Diana and Pan

84 **Gianlorenzo Bernini**
Portrait of a Gentleman

MASTER OF THE MAGI OF FABRIANO
(Fabriano 1360s–1370s)

Madonna and Child

Polychromed wood
131 cm. (51⅝ in.) high
c. 1360–1380

Provenance:

Private collection, Florence

Bibliography:

E. Neri Lusanna, "Per l'Adorazione dei Magi di Palazzo Venezia a Roma," in *Nobilis arte manus. Festschrift zum 70. Geburtstag von Antje Middeldorf Kosegarten*, ed. by B. Klein and H. Wolter-von dem Knesebeck, Dresden-Kassel, 2002, pp. 218–227

Relevant Bibliography:

R. Sassi, "Un monaco olivetano scultore," *Rivista storica benedettina*, 24, 1955, pp. 1–4

E. Neri Lusanna, "Invenzione e replica nella scultura del Trecento: il 'Maestro dei Magi di Fabriano,'" *Studi di Storia dell'Arte*, 3, 1992, pp. 45–66

___, "Per la scultura marchigiana del '300. Il Maestro dei Magi di Fabriano e il Maestro della Madonna di Campodonico," in *I Legni Devoti*, ed. by G. Donnini, Fabriano, 1994, pp. 26–38

This sculpture group of the Madonna and Child, executed in painted wood, has survived in very good condition. Mary sits on a short bench that is covered with fabric and a white cushion. She wears a long, vermilion robe with a narrow neckline and long sleeves, in addition to a cloak, which covers her head, drapes over her shoulders, and is drawn across both legs toward her left side. Her pose is strictly upright and frontal. Mary not only faces forward, but the placement of her legs and the position of her arms are almost symmetrical. Mary's face, which has the "abstract smile of an idol" (Neri Lusanna, *op. cit.*, 2002, p. 221), also conforms to this frontal positioning.

While the tips of both feet uniformly touch the corners of the trapezoidal base, which widens toward the rear, the left heel must be slightly raised, since the left thigh is positioned somewhat higher than the right thigh. The infant Jesus sits on the raised thigh; he wears a long white robe with long sleeves. With her left hand, Mary gently supports her son, while she carefully holds the base of a vessel with the fingertips of her right hand. The vessel apparently amuses the child, who grasps it gleefully with both hands. Enrica Neri Lusanna (*op. cit.*, 2002), who is responsible for the fundamental study of this sculpture, correctly remarked that the posture of the infant Jesus, in contrast to that of the Mother, is pleasingly relaxed by the playful rotation of the body. As the Child turns to the Madonna and hands her the vessel, his right leg slips out of the robe. At the same time, out of curiosity, the Child turns his head back to look at the person from whom he has received the offering. The attribute of the vessel indicates that this Madonna and Child stood in the center of a multi-figure sculptural group of the Adoration of the Magi; typically, these groups also included the three holy kings, Melchior, Caspar and Balthazar, as well as Saint Joseph.

The back of the sculpture of the Madonna and Child is relatively straight and unmodulated. This indicates that the sculpture, along with the figures of the Magi and Saint Joseph, was originally visible only from the front, and must have stood before a wall or niche. In the back the lower section is hollowed out; this is the result of the seated position, whereby the mass at the bottom is far greater than that at the top.

The figures of another such sculpture group (figs. 1–4) are to be found in the Archbishop's Palace in Fabriano, the Marches. The Madonna and Child of that group is lost; however, Neri Lusanna (*op. cit.*, 1992) has found an old photograph of it in the photo library of the Kunsthistorisches Institut in Florence (fig. 5). That Madonna and Child almost exactly matches our Madonna and Child, including their gesture, posture and drapery, as anyone who compares the two sculptures can see.

However, there are certain differences between the two Madonna and Child sculptures that only become evident upon closer inspection, and which Neri Lusanna (*op. cit.*, 2002, pp. 220–222) did not fail to notice. Most importantly, the Child from the Fabriano group is more rigidly axial, which detracts somewhat from the narrative and emotional interest of the group. Moreover, the outlines of the Madonna in the Fabriano group are somewhat less

fig. 1

fig. 2

fig. 3

fig. 4

fig. 5

lively and interesting. The differences in the articulation of the robe worn by the Infant Jesus are also instructive. In the Madonna and Child belonging to the group in Fabriano, the body of the Child is hidden behind folds, whereas in our Madonna and Child the rounded belly of the Child is clearly visible. The two Madonna figures also differ in terms of the preparation of the gesso ground for the paint layer. The statues in the Fabriano Adoration group (and therefore, presumably, the corresponding lost Madonna and Child) have a thick gesso layer, which is covered by a thinner gesso layer for the articulation of ornamentation. In the case of our Madonna and Child, the gesso layer under the paint is very thin and the work of the sculptor is not concealed, as Neri Lusanna (*op. cit.*, 2002, p. 222) has noted. With respect to its paint and the nature of its preparatory gesso ground, according to Neri Lusanna (*op. cit.*, 2002, p. 222), our Madonna and Child matches the statues of Caspar and Balthazar (fig. 6) in the Museo di Palazzo Venezia in Rome. These statues, incidentally, are very similar to the corresponding statues of the Adoration group in Fabriano, but also show subtle differences analogous to those between the Fabriano Madonna and Child and our Madonna and Child. Consequently, it can be assumed that our Madonna and Child was originally part of an Adoration group that included the two statues of the kings in the Museo di Palazzo Venezia in Rome. The figures of Joseph and Melchior, the oldest, kneeling king, which certainly belonged to this sculpture group, are lost.

fig. 6

Neri Lusanna attributed the two sculpture groups of the Adoration of the Magi in Fabriano and in New York/Rome to an unknown "Maestro dei Magi di Fabriano" (*op. cit.*, 1992, 1994, 2002). The New York/Rome group, whose gesso ground for the paint layer is finer and whose artistic quality is somewhat higher than that of the Fabriano group, is likely to have been done by the master himself, whereas a workshop was probably involved in the creation of the other group. However, there is no basis whatsoever for the attempt (Sassi, *op. cit.*) to identify the master of the group in Fabriano as the Olivetan monk and sculptor Giovanni di Bartolomeo, who is documented in Fabriano between 1365 and 1385, since no works exist by this master that could serve as a comparison. Neri Lusanna sees the "Maestro dei Magi di Fabriano" as an artistic heir to Andrea and Nino Pisano, who also worked in the Umbrian city of Orvieto from 1347–1349. A comparison of our Madonna and Child with Nino Pisano's statue of the Eucharistic Christ (Orvieto, Cathedral Museum) illustrates that the latter may have been a source of inspiration for the "Maestro dei Magi di Fabriano." Neri Lusanna has convincingly dated the two groups of the Adoration of the Kings in the 1360s and 1370s. In terms of artistic quality, the Marchigian "Maestro dei Magi di Fabriano" was certainly the equal of his Pisan contemporaries in the wake of Nino Pisano.

Gert Kreytenberg

BARTOLOMEO BON
(c. 1405–before 1467)

Hope and Charity

Istrian stone
141 cm. high; base 12 cm. high (55½ in. high; base 4¾ in. high)
1441–1445

Provenance:

Scuola Vecchia della Misericordia, Venice
Fabbrica Nuova della Misericordia, Venice
Abbazia della Misericordia, Venice
Moro-Lin family, Venice
Private collection, Ferrara

Bibliography:

F. Sansovino, *Venetia citta nobilissima e singolare*, Venice, 1581, c. 101V

F. Sansovino, *Venetia citta nobilissima e singolare*, ed. by G. Martinioni, Venice, 1663, p. 286

J. Grevembroch, *Monumenta Veneta ex antiquis ruderibus*, Vol. 2, Venice, 1754, p. 83

E. Paoletti, *Il fiore di Venezia*, III, Venice, 1840, pp. 18–20

Venezia e le sue lagune, ii, pt. 2, Venice, 1847, pp. 287–288

J. Burckhardt, *Der Cicerone*, Leipzig, 1925, pp. 585–586

J. Pope-Hennessy, *Catalogue of Italian Sculpture in the Victoria and Albert Museum*, London, 1964, no. 369, pp. 342–345

W. Wolters, *La scultura veneziana gotica (1300–1460)*, Venice, 1976, Vol. I, pp. 290–291, no. 250

A. Markham Schulz, *The Sculpture of Giovanni and Bartolomeo Bon and their Workshop*, Philadelphia, 1978, pp. 12–23

E. Martinelli Pedrocco, in *Le scuole di Venezia*, Milan, 1981, pp. 217–218, 226 nn. 5–8

A. Tambini, "La Chiesa della Croce Coperta di Lugo: alcune testimonianze artistiche del quattrocento," in *Studi Romagnoli* XLVIII, 1997, pp. 61–63

A. Zorzi, *Venezia Scomparsa*, Milan, 2001, pp. 312

Relevant Bibliography:

J. Pope-Hennessy, *Italian Gothic Sculpture*, 4th edition, London, 1996, pp. 223–225, 277–278

W. Wolters, "Bartolomeo Buon," in *The Dictionary of Art*, London, 1996, Vol. 5, pp. 176–177

Bartolomeo Bon has been described by John Pope-Hennessy as "the most important Venetian sculptor of the first half of the fifteenth century" (Pope-Hennessy, 1964, *op. cit.*, p. 342), and by Wolfgang Wolters as "the founder of Renaissance architecture in Venice" (Wolters, 1996, *op. cit.*, p. 176). Bartolomeo trained in his father Giovanni's workshop in Venice, and father and son are documented as having worked together on the Ca' d'Oro, the tympanum lunette over the entrance to the Scuola di San Marco, and the Porta della Carta, the monumental entrance to the Palazzo Ducale. Upon his father's death in 1442, Bartolomeo took over the workshop. His numerous projects included the main portals for the churches of SS. Giovanni e Paolo and the Madonna dell'Orto, and his primary architectural work, the Ca' del Duca palace on the Grand Canal.

The present statues of *Hope* and *Charity* were executed for one of Bartolomeo's most celebrated projects, the façade of the Scuola Vecchia della Misericordia in Venice, founded in 1308 and located on the northern edge of the city. On 6 August 1441 the Guild of the Misericordia (of which Bartolomeo himself was a member) agreed to reconstruct the Scuola Vecchia's façade.

Bartolomeo's sculptural program for the Scuola's façade received great praise throughout the Renaissance and is even cited in the first guidebook to the city, *Venetia città nobilissima e singolare,* published in 1581 by Francesco Sansovino, the son of Jacopo Sansovino, the sculptor, architect, and designer of the Scuola Nuova della Misericordia. Francesco states:

"Ha la fabrica vecchia sopra il portone la statua di nostra Donna di marmo, con bell'aria, belle mani, & con panni molto ben intesi, & fu scolpita da Bartolomeo che fece il Portone di Palazzo. Scolpì similmente le figure che sono nel frontispitio d'essa Scuola, . . ." (Sansovino-Martinioni, *op. cit.*, p. 286).

The "statua di nostra Donna" to which Sansovino refers is the large relief depicting the *Madonna of Mercy* now in the collection of the Victoria and Albert Museum in London (fig. 1), and the present figures of *Hope* and *Charity* were among "le figure che sono nel frontispitio."

Bon's façade sculptures were transferred to Jacopo Sansovino's Fabbrica Nuova della Misericordia in 1612, when the Scuola Vecchia was acquired by the Silkweavers' Guild. There the sculptures occupied an arched space over the central portal and were described by Martinioni in his edition of Sansovino's *Venetia,* published in 1663:

"La Statua di nostra Donna, che era sopra il Portone della fabrica Vecchia, come dice il Sansouino di sopra, stà collocata al presente sopra la porta della fabrica nuoua, doue hanno trasportato ogn'altro ornamento, che si ritrouaua in detta scuola vecchia, hauendola cessa à Tessitori di panni di seta" (Sansovino-Martinioni, *op. cit.,* p. 286)

The portal ensemble is also recorded in a drawing of 1754 by Johannes Grevembroch (fig. 2), where the figures of *Hope* and *Charity* are shown flanking the central relief of the

fig. 1

fig. 2

fig. 3

Madonna of Mercy. A figure of *Faith* surmounts the arch, while two small angels stand at its outer edges, and an inscription running along its interior edge records the date that the sculptures were transferred to the Fabbrica Nuova: 7 February 1612.

By the spring of 1834 the sculptures had been moved inside the church of the Misericordia by Abbot Pietro Pianton, who was overseeing the church's restoration. At this time the relief of the *Madonna of Mercy* was installed on the left side of the entrance end of the church, and the figures of *Faith, Hope* and *Charity* were installed opposite the relief, at the entrance to the chapel dedicated to Saint Filomena. They are described by Paoletti in this context as Saints Christina, Dorothy, and Callista, and were recorded in an engraving by Buttazzon (fig. 3).

After the death of Abbot Pianton's successor in 1868, the church was closed and the sculptures were in the possession of the Moro-Lin family of Venice.

Although the exact placement of the figures of *Hope* and *Charity* in their original context at the Scuola Vecchia della Misericordia is not recorded, Sansovino's use of the term "frontispitio" in his description is suggestive. According to the sixteenth-century *Vocabolario degli Accademici della Crusca*, the architectural term "frontispizio" can refer to the upper part of a façade, door, or window that is triangular or arched in shape. It is therefore possible that the present figures once stood over the portal and flanked the relief of the *Madonna della Misericordia* in an arrangement similar to the one installed above the door of the Fabbrica Nuova in 1612 and recorded by Grevembroch. Another possible interpretation is that they occupied the two tabernacles that surmount the upper corners of the building's arched façade as posited by Schulz (*op. cit.*, p. 17).

Jeanette Sisk

URBANO DI PIETRO
Known as URBANO DA CORTONA
(Cortona c. 1425–Siena, 1504)

Dead Christ Supported by Two Angels

Marble
57.2 x 59 cm. (22½ x 23½ in.)
c. 1450

Provenance:

Art market, Florence
Giancarlo Gallino, Turin

Bibliography:

"Urbano da Cortona," in *Dal Romanico al Rinascimento* (exh. cat., Antichi maestri pittori, Turin, 21 November–21 December 1986), Turin, 1986, n. p.

G. Gentilini, in *Dal Trecento al Seicento: le arti a paragone* (exh. cat., Antichi maestri pittori, Turin, 2 October–30 November 1991), Turin, 1991, pp. 39–45

R. Munman, "Urbano da Cortona: Corrections and Contributions," in *Verrocchio and Late Quattrocento Italian Sculpture*, Florence, 1992, pp. 238–239, fig. 192

G. Gentilini, in *Francesco di Giorgio e il Rinascimento a Siena 1450–1500*, ed. by L. Bellosi (exh. cat., Chiesa di Sant'Agostino, Siena, 25 April–31 July 1993), Milan, 1993, pp. 190, 529

Relevant Bibliography:

P. Schubring, *Urbano da Cortona,* Strassburg, 1903

H. Belting, *The image and its public in the Middle Ages: form and function of early paintings of the Passion,* trans. by M. Bartusis and R. Meyer, New Rochelle, New York, 1990

G. Gentilini and C. Sisi, *Collezione Chigi Saracini. La scultura: bozzetti in terracotta, piccoli marmi e altre sculture dal XIV al XX secolo* (exh. cat., Palazzo Chigi Saracini, Siena, 1989), Florence, 1989

S. Magliani, "Cattedrale di San Lorenzo: la decorazione plastica nel Quattrocento," in *Una città e la sua cattedrale. Il duomo di Perugia*, ed. by M. L. Cianini Pierotti, Perugia, 1992, pp. 295–314

G. Bonsanti, in *Donatello e i suoi*, ed. by A. P. Darr and G. Bonsanti (exh. cat., Forte di Belvedere, Florence, 15 June–7 September 1986), Detroit and Milan, 1986, p. 160

V. Herzner, "Donatello in Siena," in *Mitteilungen des Kunsthistorischen Institutes in Florenz*, xv, 1971, pp. 161–186

M. Scalini, "L'armatura fiorentina del Quattrocento e la produzione d'armi in Toscana," in *Guerra e guerrieri nella Toscana del Rinascimento*, ed. by F. Cardini and M. Tangheroni, Florence, 1990, pp. 83-126

L. Puppi, "Osservazioni sui riflessi dell'arte di Donatello tra Padova e Ferrara," in *Donatello e il suo tempo. Atti dell'VIII Convegno internazionale di studi sul Rinascimento*, Florence-Padua, 25 September–1 October 1966, Florence, 1968, pp. 307-329

J. D. Draper, in *Donatello e i suoi*, ed. by A. P. Darr and G. Bonsanti (exh. cat., Forte di Belvedere, Florence, 15 June–7 September 1986), Detroit and Milan, 1986, pp. 257–258, n. 107

V. Krahn, *Bartolomeo Bellano, Studien zur Paduaner Plastik des Quattrocento*, Munich, 1988

fig. 1

This image shows the Dead Christ, visible from the waist up in the tomb, with his hands crossed on his stomach (originally the backs of his hands likely had a representation of the wounds from the nails in paint), in keeping with the traditional iconography of the *Imago Pietatis* (Belting, *op. cit.*). He is supported on each side by two angels represented in mirror image to each other. Like the Christ, the two angels emerge from the tomb, of which the frontal part is divided into four quadrangles containing stylized roses with long jagged leaves.

The image is enclosed within a slightly concave roundel framed by a molding. On both the top and the bottom of the roundel, a second short, straight line of molding begins but is abruptly interrupted. This detail suggests that the sculpture was the central image of a panel composed of three flanking elements that were carved separately—perhaps a rectangular altar-frontal that included two lateral panels. This would have been framed by the moldings that here bend to accommodate the relief, and circumscribed by the cornice, of which only two portions are now visible. On the back the stone is heavily and summarily hewed, and reveals two lateral notches used to secure two marble plates of a similar width. The marble employed is pale, yellowish-gray, variegated and veined; it is of a kind readily found in the Sienese region—possibly the so-called "gray marble of the Montagnola" (a quarry near Siena). This was frequently used by Sienese sculptors during the fifteenth century, who liked its austere coloring, somewhat reminiscent of archaeological remains. The block shows a few abrasions, particularly at the bottom, most likely due to its original location, probably below an altar.

This image is deliberately simplified in compositional terms, and is carved in a somewhat anti-naturalistic manner that plays on archaic elements suggestive of traditional iconography in Medieval and Byzantine art. It recalls ivory sculpture of late antiquity, and yet reveals a more modern and relaxed element in its suggestion of benevolent humanity. Note, for example, Christ's melancholy expression, and the loving and reassuring gesture of the angels who, in spite of their starched robes, lean their heads forward to exchange compassionate gazes.

The attribution of this relief to Urbano da Cortona has recently been confirmed by Robert Munman (*op. cit.*), and there is no reason to doubt it. Credible comparisons have already been made with the reliefs of the dismembered chapel of the Madonna delle Grazie, the monumental *sacellum* of the cathedral of Siena, executed by Urbano in collaboration with his brother Bartolomeo mainly between October 1451 and 1459 (but seemingly completed after 1467). The compositional abstraction, the treatment of the faces, with eyes very close together and streaked wavy hair, the robes with dotted necklines and fluted sleeves, the regular and simplified draping, and the halos resembling heavy disks that appear in this work are typical motifs that feature consistently in works by this sculptor. Munman published a hexagonal relief by the artist of an analogous subject (Dead Christ between the Virgin and Saint John; fig. 1) that had been integrated with a seventeenth-cen-

tury altar in the church of Malamerenda near Siena—a work that, in combination with the Madonna from the Chigi Saracini collection, must originally have had a similar location to that which we suggest for the present work (Gentilini, 1989, *op. cit.*, p. 64). This work also provides a relevant comparison for the entire figure of Christ.

The absence of documentation for Urbano's work makes his chronology difficult to establish, but we can see that the forms in the Dead Christ of Malamerenda are more frail, angular and sinewy, closer in style to the tomb of Bishop Andrea Baglioni, executed by Urbano for the Cathedral of Perugia between 1450 and the early months of the following year (Magliani, *op. cit.*). However, in this case a greater formal breadth is reminiscent of the Virtues of the bench in the Loggia della Mercanzia, dated 1462, or the Madonna and Child and the symbol of the Evangelist Matthew at the Opera del Duomo, which are among the last works in marble executed by Urbano for the chapel of the Madonna delle Grazie (possibly dated after 1467). It should be noted, furthermore, that the sleeve of the angel on the right has two borders (one is near his armpit) like the left-hand angel in the lunette of Santa Caterina in Fontebranda, documented to 1470.

The present work differs from the Malamerenda relief especially in the detail of Christ's hands: small, narrow and pointed in the latter, they are exaggeratedly strong and swollen in the former, losing the anatomical accuracy that was present in the Malamerenda relief (such as in the representation of veins and knuckles). We are tempted to suggest that the larger hands denote a later execution, conforming to a more monumental and streamlined style, and perhaps the swollen, inert hands in the foreground were inspired by the Madonna del Perdono, a work sometimes said to be from Donatello's workshop, and on one occasion even attributed to Urbano himself (Bonsanti, *op. cit.*). According to recent research this work can be dated around 1457 (Herzner, *op. cit.*, pp. 167–172). But an identical representation of the hands is already visible in works that can be attributed to Urbano and executed prior to that year, such as the tombstones for Captain Henry of Nassau (who died in 1451) in the collegiate church of San Quirico d'Orcia (Scalini, *op. cit.*, pp. 106–107), for the rector Pietro Bulgarini (who died in 1456) in the atrium of Santa Maria della Scala, and, more or less contemporary, for the monk Michele Bellucci in Sant'Agostino in Massa Marittima, and the physician Luca di Simone (dated 1448) in Santa Maria Nuova in Perugia.

Our relief is of special interest for its iconography, practically unprecedented in Tuscan sculpture of the Quattrocento. The *Imago Pietatis* with angels is, however, widely found in the art of the Veneto region during this period, both in numerous pictorial representations—with several celebrated ones—and some sculptural ones, many of which have been studied by Lionello Puppi (*op. cit.*). It is likely, therefore, that Urbano imported this idea from Padua, where in 1447 he was one of Donatello's assistants working on the bronze panels for the high altar of the Santo with musician angels and symbols of the Evangelists (of the surviving works, only the angel with mandolin, I believe, can be attributed to

Urbano, and more doubtfully, the symbol of Matthew, as already pointed out by Schubring).

In the context of sculpture, the first and most noteworthy example of such a Dead Christ with angels is obviously the celebrated bronze panel for the high altar of the Santo, which, according to documents, was executed in the spring of 1449 by Donatello himself, but was in fact probably a collaborative work. Urbano does not seem to have been influenced by it, and perhaps he had not seen it as he remained in Padua only until June 1447; indeed the only common element between that and the present sculpture are the closed eyelids of Christ, which reveal the pressure of the eyes from underneath, a detail which is not unique to the Padua bronze, and could derive from other works by Donatello.

The strictly frontal view of Christ and especially the motion of the hair suggest that Urbano was familiar with another bronze Pietà from the circle of Donatello, now at the National Gallery in Washington. This is sometimes attributed to Bellano and dated towards the end of the fifteenth century (Draper, *op. cit.*), but is in fact the work of another artist active in Padua (Krahn, *op. cit.*, pp. 108–111), who, I believe, was much closer to the circle of the high altar of the Santo. It is interesting to observe that within the Sienese region there is a second example, even more explicitly reminiscent of this work: the little bronze door of a marble tabernacle in the Cathedral of Sovana, where Urbano worked around 1469, which, in its ornamentation and in the details of some of the figures, is close to Urbano's workshop.

Giancarlo Gentilini

GIOVANNI ANTONIO AMADEO
(Pavia c. 1447–Milan 1522)

Pietà

Marble
35.8 x 26.7 x 11 cm. (14⅛ x 10⅝ x 4¼ in.)
c. 1465–1475

Provenance:

Private collection, Florence

Bibliography:

F. Petrucci, in *Italian Sculpture: from the Gothic to the Baroque*, ed. by A. Butterfield and A. Radcliffe (exh. cat., Salander-O'Reilly Galleries, New York, 4 December 2002–1 February 2003), New York, 2002, pp. 94–98

S. Douglas, review of the exhibition "Italian Sculpture: from the Gothic to the Baroque," Salander-O'Reilly Galleries, 4 December 2002–1 February 2003, in *The Art Newspaper*, "What's On," December 2002, p. 4

S. Masoero, review of the exhibition "Italian Sculpture: from the Gothic to the Baroque," Salander-O'Reilly Galleries, 4 December 2002–1 February 2003, in *Sole 24 Ore*, 19 January 2003

P. Jeromack, review of the exhibition "Italian Sculpture: from the Gothic to the Baroque," Salander-O'Reilly Galleries, 4 December 2002–1 February 2003, in *Art & Auction*, "Datebook," February 2003, pp. 113–114

Relevant Bibliography:

F. Malaguzzi Valeri, *Gio. Antonio Amadeo. Scultore e architetto lombardo (1447–1522)*, Bergamo, 1904

E. Arslan, "Amadeo," in *Dizionario Biografico degli Italiani*, Rome, 1960

C. Angelini, M. G. Albertini Ottolenghi, R. Bossaglia, and F. Renzo Pesenti, *La Certosa di Pavia*, Milan, 1968

Giovanni Antonio Amadeo. I Documenti, ed. by Richard V. Schofield, Janice Shell, and Grazioso Sironi, Como, 1989

C. Morscheck, "Francesco Solari: Amadeo's Master," in *Giovanni Antonio Amadeo, Scultura e Architettura del suo tempo*, ed. by J. Shell and L. Castelfranchi, Milan, 1993, pp. 103–23

A. Butterfield, "Antonio Rossellino, *St. Jerome in the Wilderness*," in *Masterpieces of Renaissance Art: Eight Rediscoveries* (exh. cat., Salander-O'Reilly Galleries, New York, 29 November 2001– 2 February 2002), New York, 2001, pp. 20–31

J. D. Draper, in *The Metropolitan Museum of Art Bulletin*, Vol. LX, no. 2, 2002, p. 14

fig. 1

Since publication of this sculpture in 2002, additional information has come to light that both confirms the attribution of the work to Amadeo and expands understanding of its original artistic context and function. Given the great importance and beauty of this work, it merits presenting here a further account of the sculpture.

Scholarship on Lombard Renaissance sculpture is in an inchoate state, despite the recent efforts of Bernstein, Casciaro, Morscheck, Schofield, Shell, and many others. Yet as any visitor to the Museo del Duomo in Milan can see, the achievements of Giovanni Antonio Amadeo, Solari, and the Mantegazza brothers rivaled those of sculptors in Venice and Florence (with the obvious exception of Michelangelo) in beauty, inventiveness and classicism. The case of Amadeo is particularly noteworthy.

Amadeo was perhaps the most important sculptor in Milan and Lombardy during the second half of the fifteenth century. His principal sculptural projects include the Monument of Medea Colleoni, the Chapel of Bartolomeo Colleoni, and the sculpture of the façade of the Certosa of Pavia, the execution of which he divided with Antonio and Cristoforo Mantegazza. Amadeo also played a leading role as an architect. The Colleoni Chapel was a particularly influential model in Lombard northern Italy. In addition, Amadeo collaborated with Bramante on the tribune of Santa Maria delle Grazie, Milan, and served as the *capomaestro*, or chief architect, of the Duomo of Milan.

The present work depicts the Pietà: the Virgin Mary holds her dead son upright on her lap. With her right hand she lovingly supports his head; one lock of his hair is held between the index and middle fingers of her hand. With her left hand she grasps his body around his thigh; such is the force of her grip that folds of his loincloth bulge between her fingers. Her hands are exquisitely carved and finely detailed. A vein courses the back of her left hand; a vein bifurcates over the bone in her right hand. Dressed in a hood and wimple, she is wearing the costume of a religious. Her expression is one of intense grief; her features are almost like those of an old man. The physiognomy of her body is distinctive. Her torso is long, her bony knees jut forward, and her arms are unnaturally long.

The figure of Christ is of surpassing beauty. His legs and torso are very finely formed; the bones of his ribs and clavicle delicately stand out in shallow relief. His features are noble, and his beard and hair are exquisitely carved. Especially noteworthy are the drilling and undercutting of his curly locks. His proportions are striking: his body suggests the forms of both an adult and a child. This was perhaps calculated to increase our sense of his mother's loss. Also remarkable are the evident optical corrections in the carving of his torso: it is foreshortened, in three-quarter view, and takes into account the *dal dì sotto in su* vantage of the viewer.

The figures are posed on a steeply inclined projection that juts forward, beyond the carved engaged frame surrounding the relief. There is only one other known marble that shares this feature: the marble relief of Saint Jerome in the Metropolitan Museum of Art,

formerly published as by Antonio Rossellino but subsequently attributed to Benedetto da Maiano by James David Draper (Butterfield, *op. cit.*; Draper, *op. cit.*). Interestingly, the two reliefs are of approximately the same date.

In the present work, the landscape behind the figures is carved in very low relief. At the right, in the upper corner, a turreted castle surmounts a hill. The style of the architecture of this edifice is unmistakably Lombard and fifteenth-century. A rider on horseback approaches the castle. Near the lower right corner, a young branch in leaf extends from a cut tree.

The carving of the sculpture is of exceptionally fine quality, and the image is full of affective details, seemingly for the viewer's contemplation. These facts, combined with the intimate scale of the sculpture, establish beyond doubt that the relief was intended for private meditation and devotion. It was a common feature of prayer in the Renaissance that, often in conjunction with works of art, the devout imagined the figures of religious history acquiring bodily form before their eyes. This practice was especially recommended in meditation upon scenes of the life of Christ, from his Passion above all. This knowledge perhaps helps us to understand the dramatic projection of the figures beyond the containing frame of the sculpture.

In quality and detail, there are few parallels anywhere in Renaissance art for this outstanding sculpture. It is likely that a work of such distinction was made for an exceptional patron, someone like Bartolomeo Colleoni or Gianfrancesco Sforza. Although there is no direct way to prove this attractive hypothesis, it is the case that works of such quality were not commissioned by patrons of lesser wealth and status.

That Amadeo is the author of this extraordinary sculpture can be made abundantly clear through comparison with other known works, mostly from the early part of his career. One key reference point is the Colleoni Chapel in Bergamo, a commission that is documented to the artist between 1470 and 1475. The present relief bears unmistakable similarities in composition, style, and execution to much of Amadeo's work there. Especially comparable are the reliefs depicting the *Carrying of the Cross*, the *Crucifixion* (fig. 1, detail), and the *Deposition* (fig. 2) from the lower sarcophagus of Bartolomeo Colleoni.

The group of three mourning women in the foreground of the *Crucifixion* panel shows general similarities to the Virgin in the present relief, particularly in the manner in which the folds of their veils frame their faces. In addition, elements of the Virgin Mary's costume in the *Crucifixion* panel are highly similar to those in the present relief, notably, the high-belted dress with long, close-fitting sleeves, the cloak folded back over the shoulders, and the disposition of the drapery across the Virgin's knees.

There are even closer points of comparison between the *Deposition* in the Colleoni Chapel and the present relief. The positioning of the figures of the Virgin and Christ is closely similar in the two examples. However, in the Colleoni *Deposition* the body of Christ

fig. 2

is laid out more horizontally, and the Virgin leans toward him with more urgency, reflecting the extreme drama of the narrative scene. In the present relief the body of Christ is more upright and the expression and posture of Mary more restrained, in keeping with the contemplative nature of the work.

The physiognomy, anatomy, and costume of the figures are highly similar in both works. The facial features of Christ, as well as the delicate drilling and undercutting of his hair and beard, are nearly identical in appearance, and the Virgin's face shows an expression of grief and mourning in both sculptures. Equally comparable in the two reliefs are the ripples in the fabric of the Virgin's sleeve as it clings to her delicately curving arm; her cloak, fastened at the neck and turned back over her shoulder; and the arrangement of the drapery as it falls from her knees, which project strongly into the foreground.

The treatment of space in the two reliefs is also alike, with a marked contrast between the foreground figures carved in exceptionally high relief, and the background in very low relief. Furthermore, as in the Colleoni *Deposition*, a projecting ledge of craggy rockery runs along the lower front edge of the *Pietà*.

In the Small Cloister of the Certosa of Pavia, there is a sculpture of the *Pietà* (fig. 3) on a capital that is commonly referred to by art historians as West 4 and traditionally attributed to Amadeo. The capital is in a rougher, cheaper and more porous stone than the present relief, but the many points of similarity are indisputable, including the pose of the figures, the costume and drapery of the Madonna, and Christ's head, beard, legs and feet.

There are at least three other works by or attributed to Amadeo at the Certosa of Pavia that bear a very strong resemblance to the present sculpture. One is the *Annunciation* in terracotta in the lavabo of the Small Cloister, a documented work by the artist. As in the present sculpture, there the Madonna's left arm is notably long, and the sleeve has extremely similar folds.

Another similar work is the roundel of St. Gregory in the *tiburio* of the church, recently attributed to Amadeo (See Morscheck, *op. cit.*, esp. p. 120, fig. 11), in which the folds in St. Gregory's cloak spread and turn from the clasp high on his chest in a manner similar to that in the Madonna's costume in the present relief.

The third is the marble relief over

fig. 3

the Portal of the Small Cloister, signed by Amadeo and dated to c. 1466–1469. In the present sculpture Christ and the Madonna are older figures, and in the relief in the tympanum of the portal they are young. Nevertheless, in both works the structure of the Madonna's body is the same: she has a notably long torso; and her knees are positioned relatively low in relation to her upper body and project forward to form a kind of shelf or plateau. Furthermore, in both sculptures the knees press up pointedly against the drapery, which falls in sharply angled furrows that spread downward from the knees, terminating in a pile of faceted folds at her feet. Additionally, in both works the belt is secured high on the Madonna's body, and the folds of her tunic are gathered and radiate from underneath the belt.

The figures in the architrave of the portal also display many points of comparison with the present relief, including the proper left arm of the angel on the right in the Man of Sorrows with Angels over the center of the door. Like the left arm of the Madonna, that limb is long and reticulated, and the sleeve is divided into a series of highly comparable folds. The face of the bishop to the left of this group also bears a general similarity to that of the Madonna.

There is another comparable autograph work by Amadeo to consider, the relief of St. Jerome in the Duomo in Cremona. Like the Portal of the Small Cloister, it is signed and it is dated 1484. In this work, the particular point of comparison is the anatomy of St. Jerome, and especially of his upper torso, neck and shoulders. These passages are unmistakably analogous to the same areas of the body of Christ in the *Pietà*.

Andrew Butterfield

BENEDETTO DA MAIANO
(Maiano 1441–Florence 1497)

Head of a Man (Giovanni Serristori?)

Terracotta
27 x 19 x 22 cm. (10⅝ x 7½ x 8¾ in.)
c. 1475

Provenance:

Private Collection, United Kingdom (?); Sale, Sotheby's London,
  9 April 1981, lot 106
Private collection, Berlin
Private collection, Montana, Switzerland
Sascha Mehringer, Munich

Related Bibliography:

C. Gilbert, in *Italian Art 1400–1500: Sources and Documents*,
New Jersey, 1980, pp. 42–47, esp. p. 47 (annotated translation of
the inventory of Benedetto da Maiano's studio)

A. Radcliffe, in *The Thyssen-Bornemisza Collection: Renaissance
and later sculpture with works of art in bronze*, London, 1992,
pp. 62–67, no. 4

J. Pope-Hennessy, *Italian Renaissance Sculpture,* 4th ed., London,
1996, pp. 186, 188–189, 381–382, pls. 176–177

B. Boucher, *Earth and Fire: Italian Terracotta Sculpture from
Donatello to Canova* (exh. cat., Museum of Fine Arts, Houston,
18 November 2001–3 February 2002; Victoria and Albert
Museum, 14 March 2001–7 July 2002), New Haven and
London, 2001, pp. 142–145, nos. 18, 19

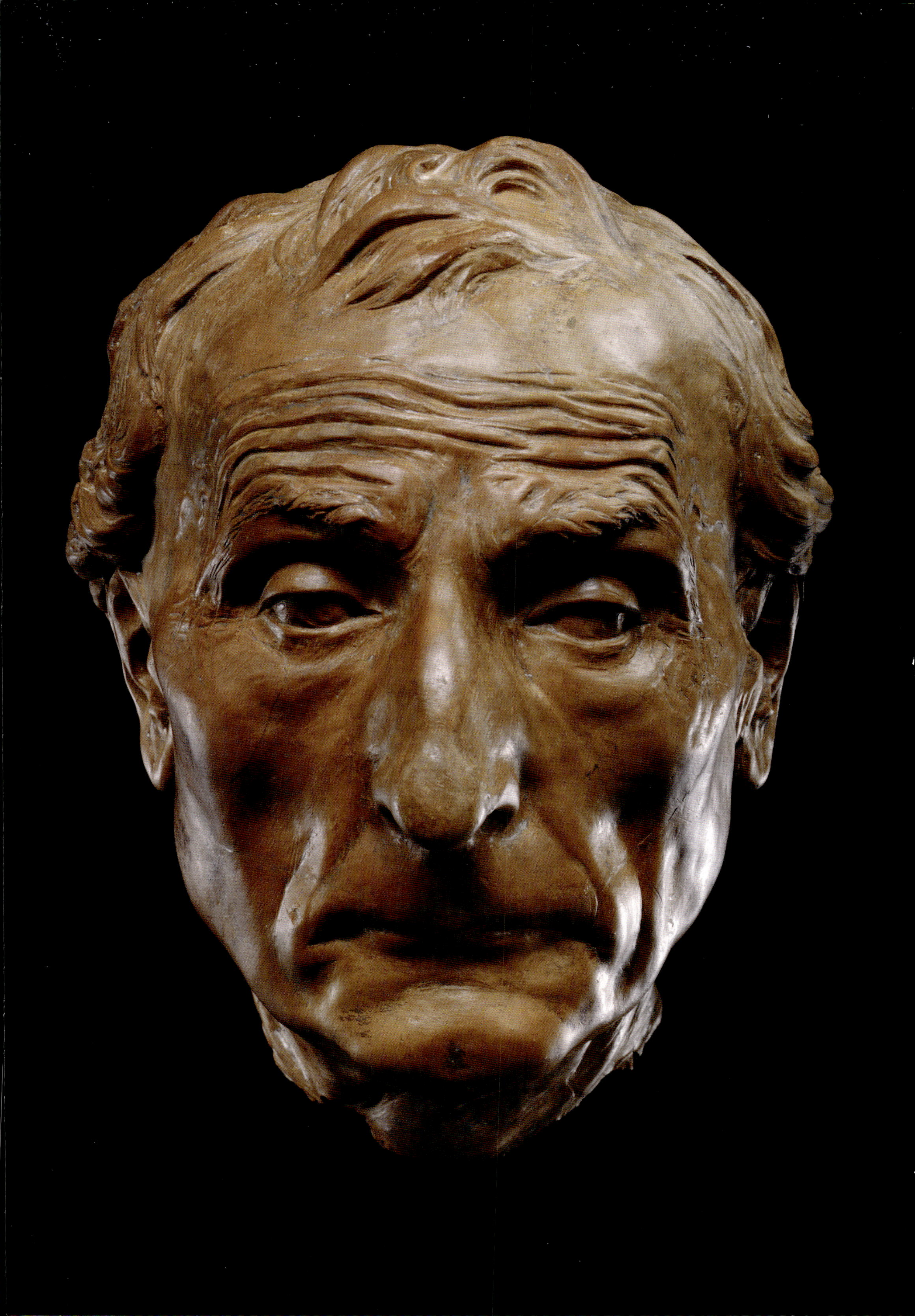

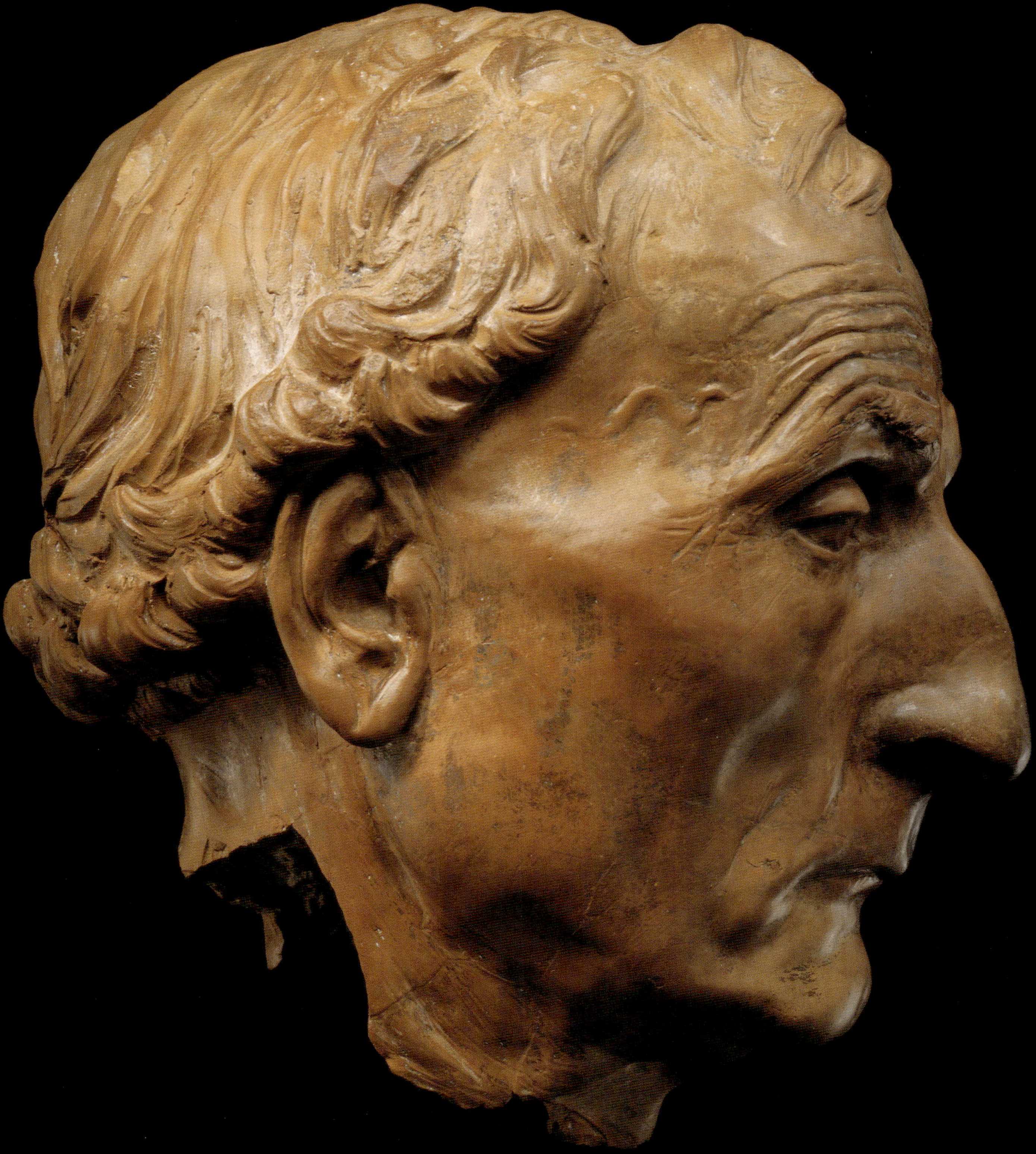

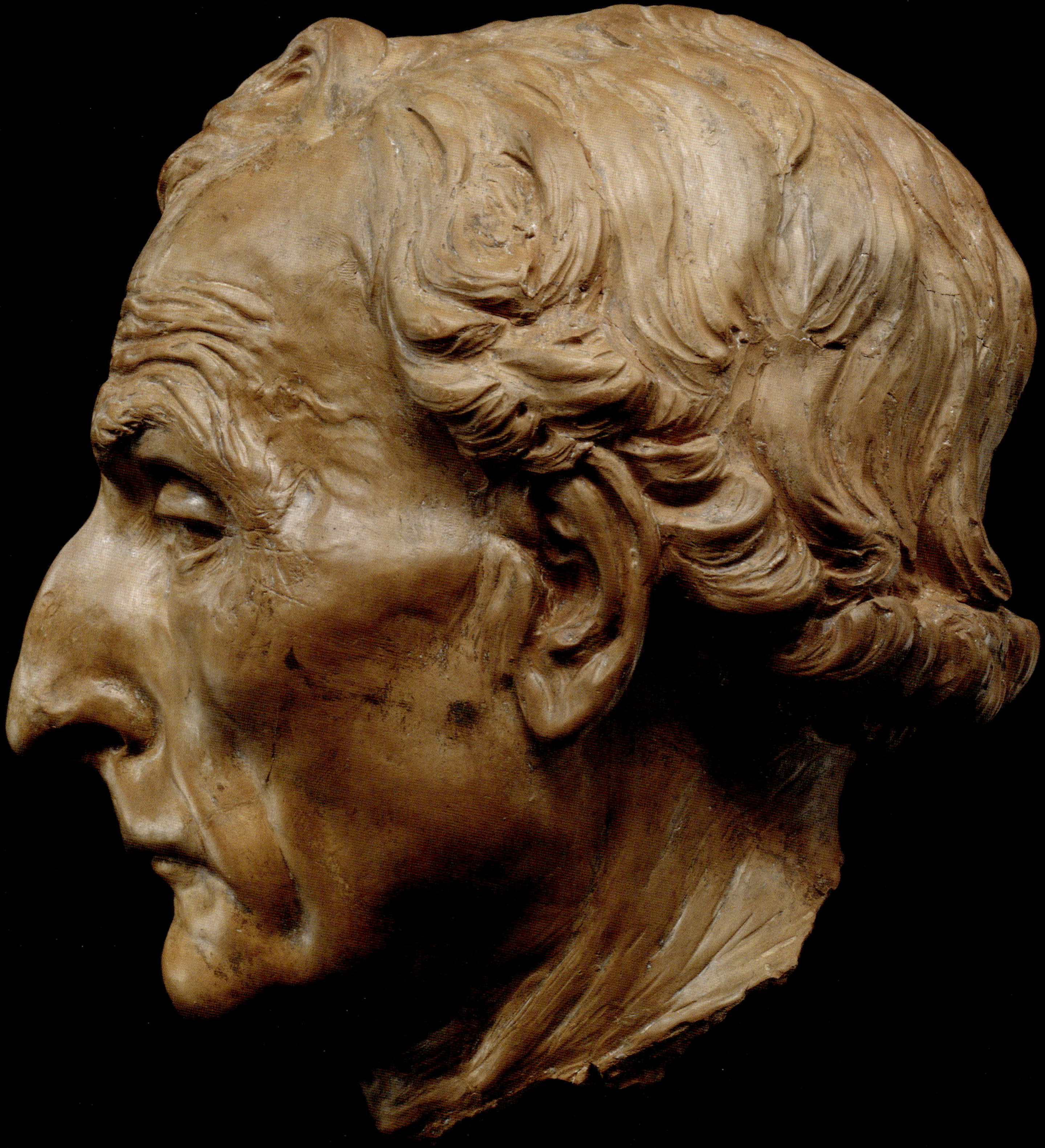

Although this sculpture is previously unpublished, its attribution to Benedetto da Maiano is confirmed by the many details of the head that exactly correspond with features in Benedetto's other sculptures and, above all, in his portrait busts. For example, the treatment of the muscles under the eyes and above the cheekbones is virtually the same as in the terracotta model for the bust of Filippo Strozzi (1475; fig. 1), in the Staatliche Museen zu Berlin. Other points of close comparison with the Strozzi terracotta bust are the shape of the ears and the form of the chin, and especially the subtly indicated dimple in the chin.

fig. 1

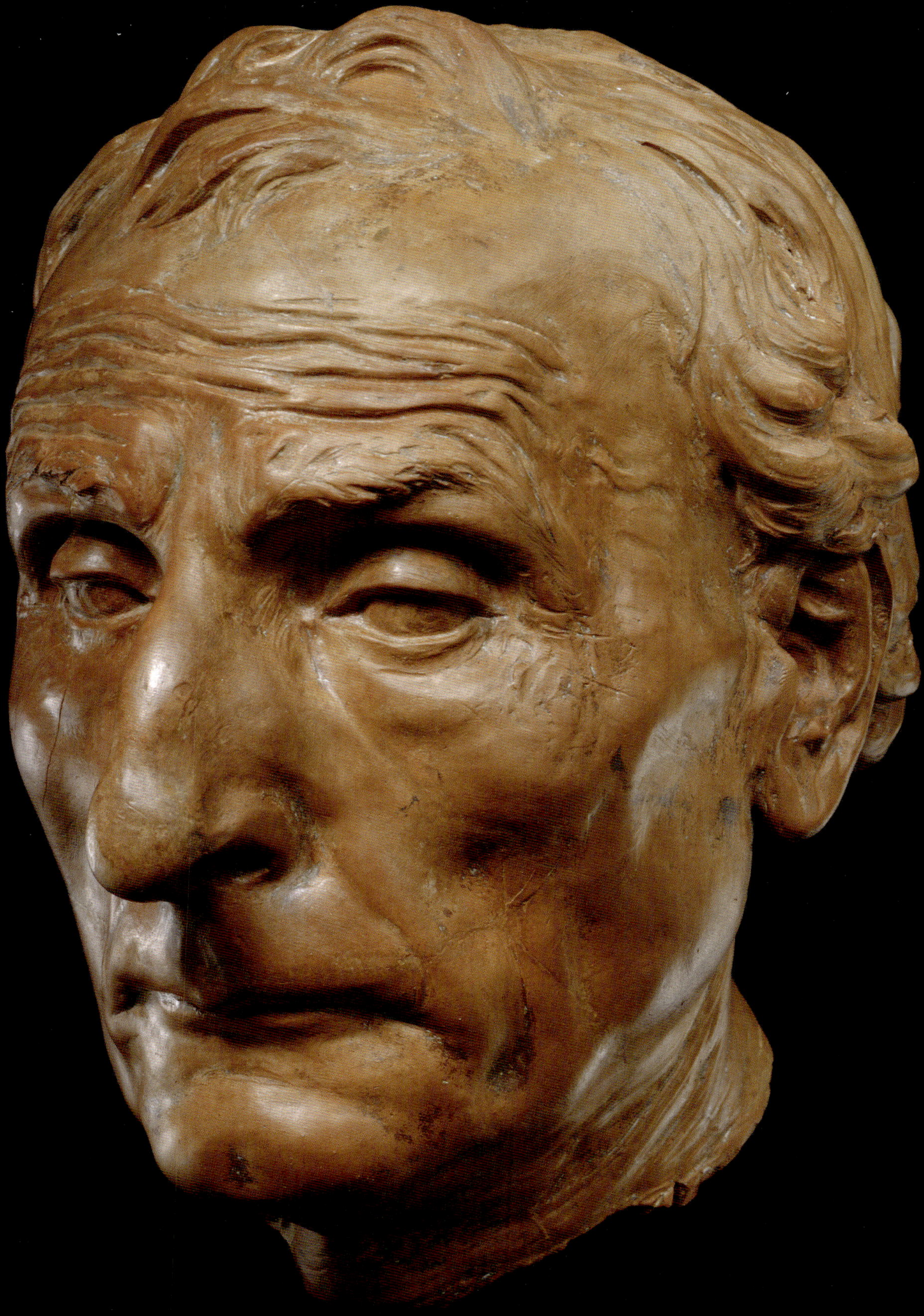

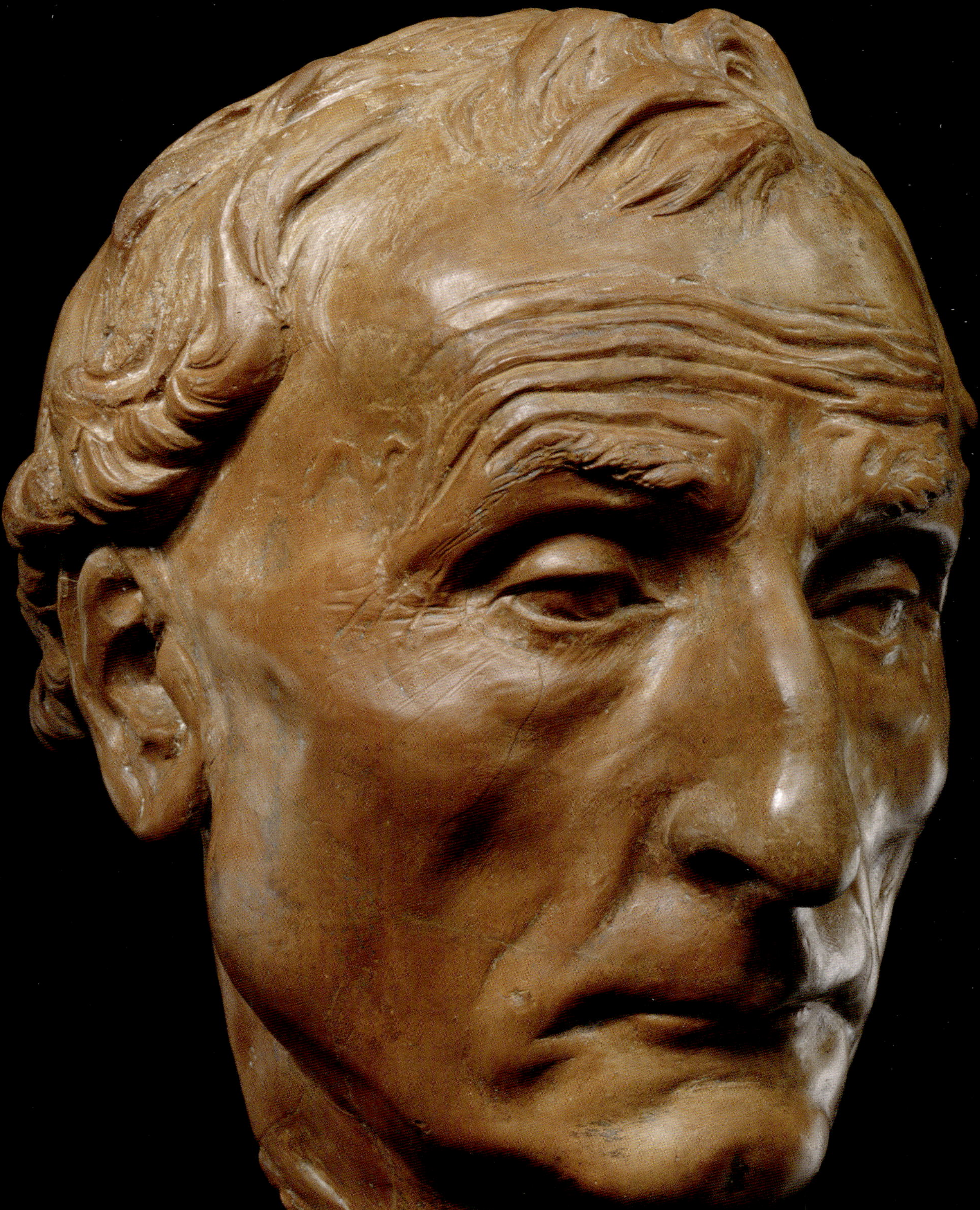

A multitude of extremely similar correspondences can also be found in Benedetto da Maiano's marble bust of Pietro Mellini (1474; fig. 2), in the Bargello. In both sculptures, a complex network of wrinkles gives character to the forehead of the figure. In both, the ridges of the eye-sockets are strongly indicated and form relatively sharp angles at the outer corners. In both, the skin around the ears is creased, and the skin of the neck gently sags. The treatment of the musculature of the mouth, jaw and chin is also highly comparable in the two works. Furthermore, one should note the small circular indentation near the proper right corner of the mouth of our bust. This marks the former site of a mole that has subsequently been damaged and lost. The Mellini bust has a mole in nearly the same location.

fig. 2

One should also note the points of resemblance of the present work to Benedetto da Maiano's terracotta model of Saint John the Evangelist, in the Thyssen collection. The modeling of the area above the nose and between the eyebrows is unmistakably similar in the two sculptures. Also comparable are the form of the cheekbones and the shape of the ears.

Benedetto made the bust of Pietro Mellini in 1474 and the bust of Filippo Strozzi in 1475. Given the especially strong similarities with these two works, the present work is likely also to have been made in the middle 1470s.

The vivid, naturalistic and highly detailed character of the head indicates that it is a portrait. Unquestionably, this sculpture once formed or was intended to form the head of a terracotta model for a marble portrait bust that was either never completed or has subsequently been lost. In the terracotta model for the marble bust of Filippo Strozzi, the head was made separately from the body and then joined to the body. It is possible that the present head, too, was originally modeled separately from the rest of the bust it was made for.

The inventory of the contents of Benedetto da Maiano's studio at his death lists a terracotta head of Giovanni Serristori. It is possible that the present work is the head mentioned in that inventory (Gilbert, *op. cit.*). Giovanni Serristori (1419–1494) was an important merchant and politician in the circle of the Medici, and his mother was Costanza de' Medici. Among his many positions in the government, he was one of the twelve Buonomini, the Maestro di Zecca per l'Arte de' Mercatanti, one of the Dieci di Balìa and the Gonfaloniere di Giustizia. Given his birthdate of 1419, the apparent age of the sitter in our sculpture corresponds with the age of Giovanni Serristori at the time of its creation, c. 1475.

Writing of the Pietro Mellini bust, John Pope-Hennessy commented, "the surface . . . is treated with consummate mastery, and is inspired by a wealth of human feeling and a rich compassion which lift it to the front rank of portraiture" (Pope-Hennessy, *op. cit.*, p. 186). The present work, too, manifests an extraordinarily fine grasp of naturalistic detail combined with a deep and sympathetic representation of the inner character of the man portrayed.

Andrew Butterfield

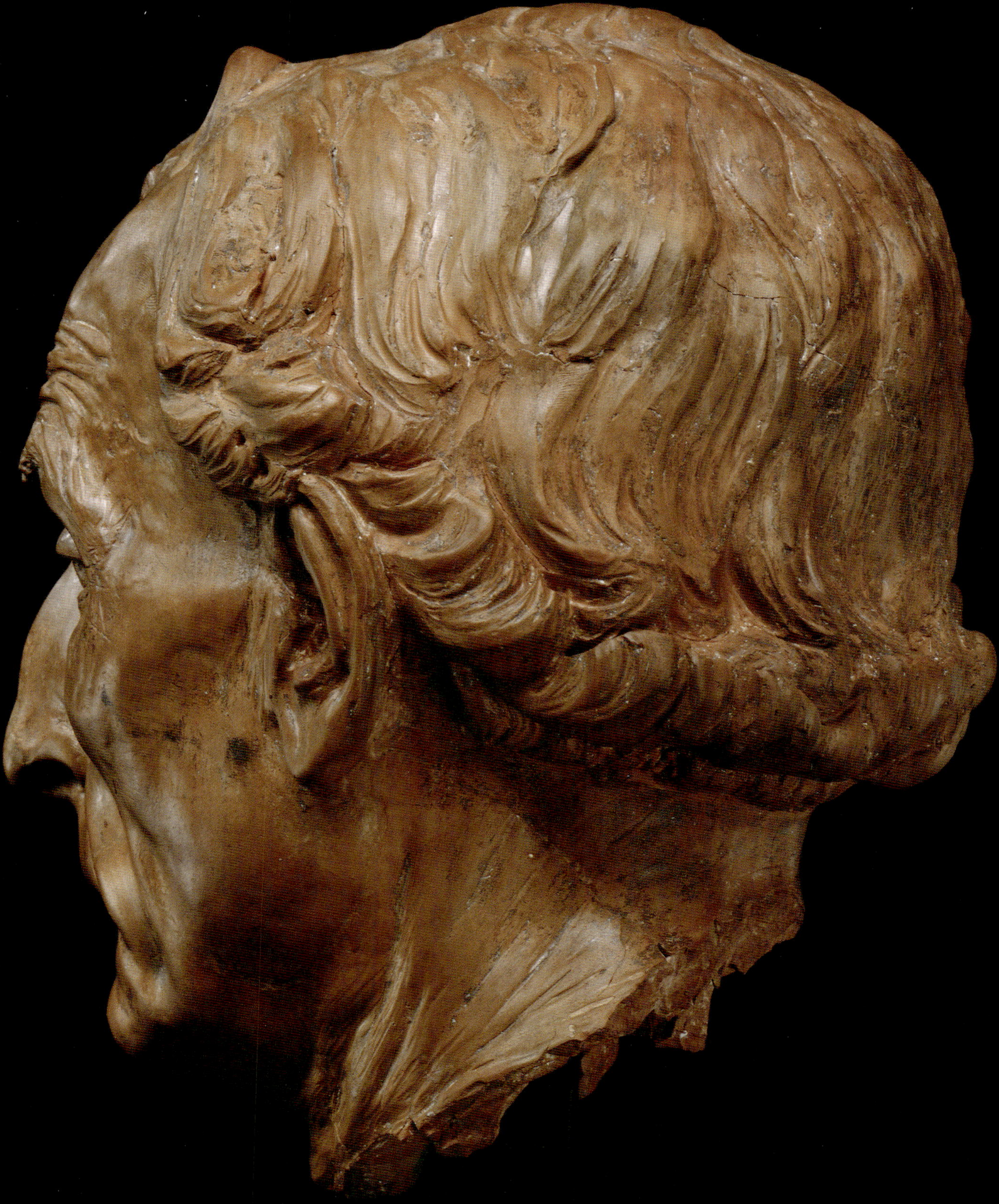

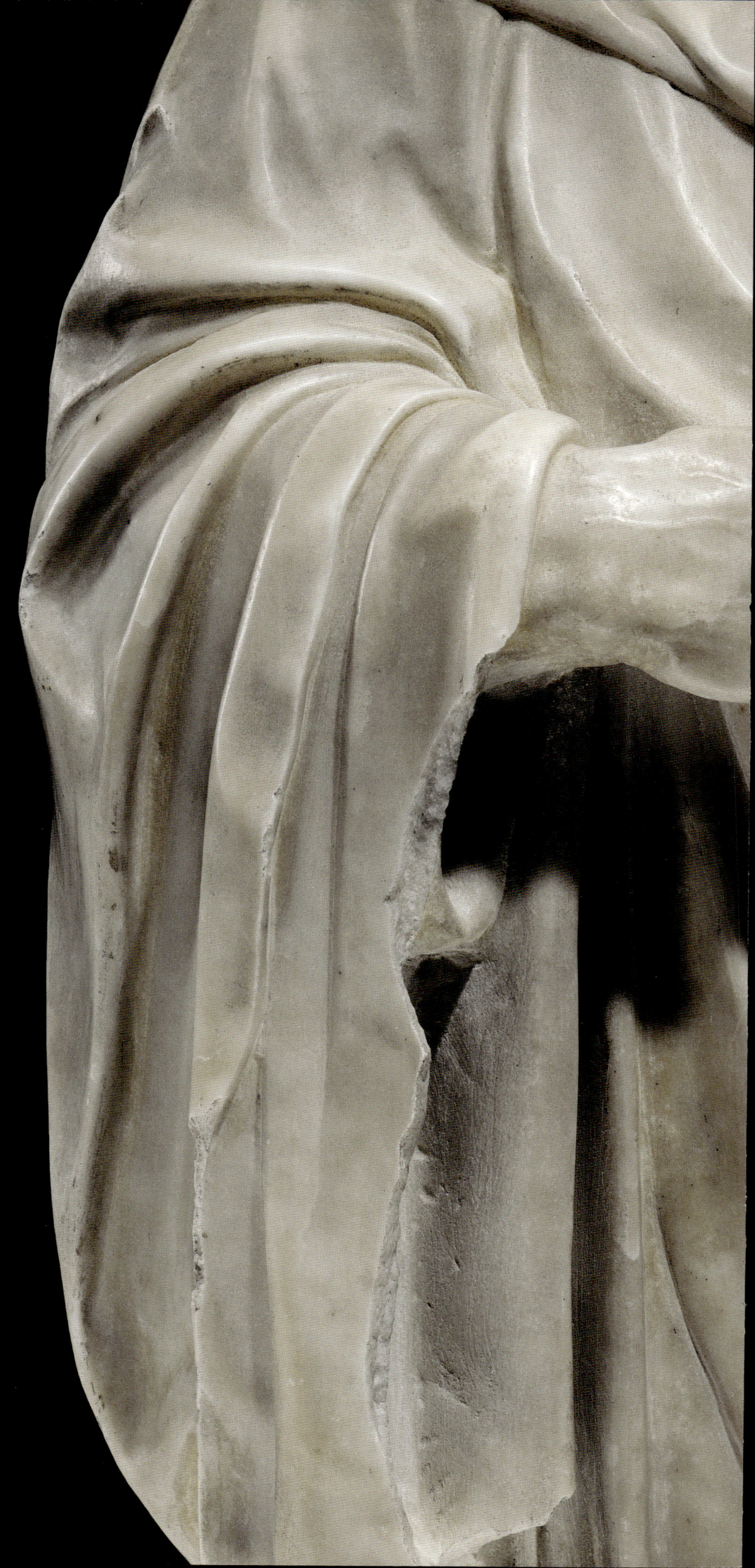

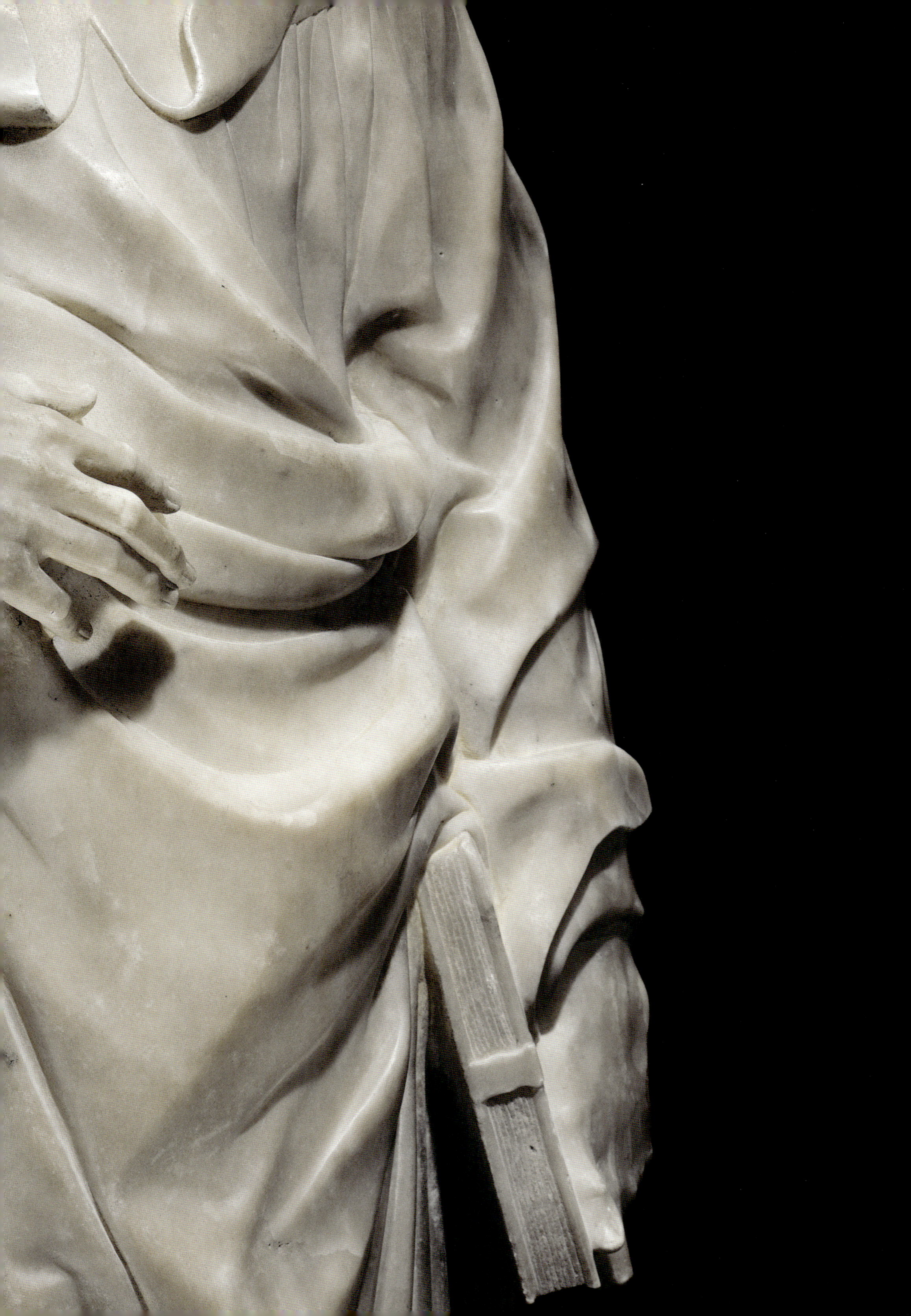

GIROLAMO SANTACROCE
(Naples c. 1502–c. 1537)

Saint John the Baptist and Saint Benedict

Marble
Saint John the Baptist: 93 cm. (36⅝ in.)
Saint Benedict: 95 cm. (37⅜ in.)
c. 1519–1520

Provenance:

High altar, Church of San Benedetto, Capua (until c. 1806–1815)
Private collection, United Kingdom

Relevant Bibliography:

R. Orsini, "La chiesa e badia di S. Benedetto e le sue vicende attraverso i secoli (1928–1929)," in *Ristampe capuane*, ed. by R. Chillemi, Capua-Naples, 1986, pp. 219–237

R. Chillemi, "Fatti e misfatti storico-artistici in un commento inedito alla Storia sacra di Capua," *Capys. Bollettino interno degli «Amici di Capua»*, 13, 1980, pp. 20–38

F. Ruotolo, "Il tempio di San Benedetto in Capua," *Capys. Bollettino interno degli «Amici di Capua»*, 16, 1983, pp. 103–114

R. Naldi, "Su Giovan Giacomo da Brescia e la bottega napoletana dell'Ordoñez: la 'cona' della cappella arcivescovile di Capua," *Prospettiva*, 81, 1996, pp. 31–51

___, *Girolamo Santacroce, orafo e scultore napoletano del Cinquecento*, Naples, 1997

___, "Giovanni da Nola 'per concorrenza di' Girolamo Santacroce: un 'Battista' nello Schloss di Vaduz," *Prospettiva*, 89–90, 1998, pp. 161–168

F. Amirante, "La scultura del '500 in Terra di Lavoro," Ph. D. diss., Seconda Università degli Studi di Napoli, 2001

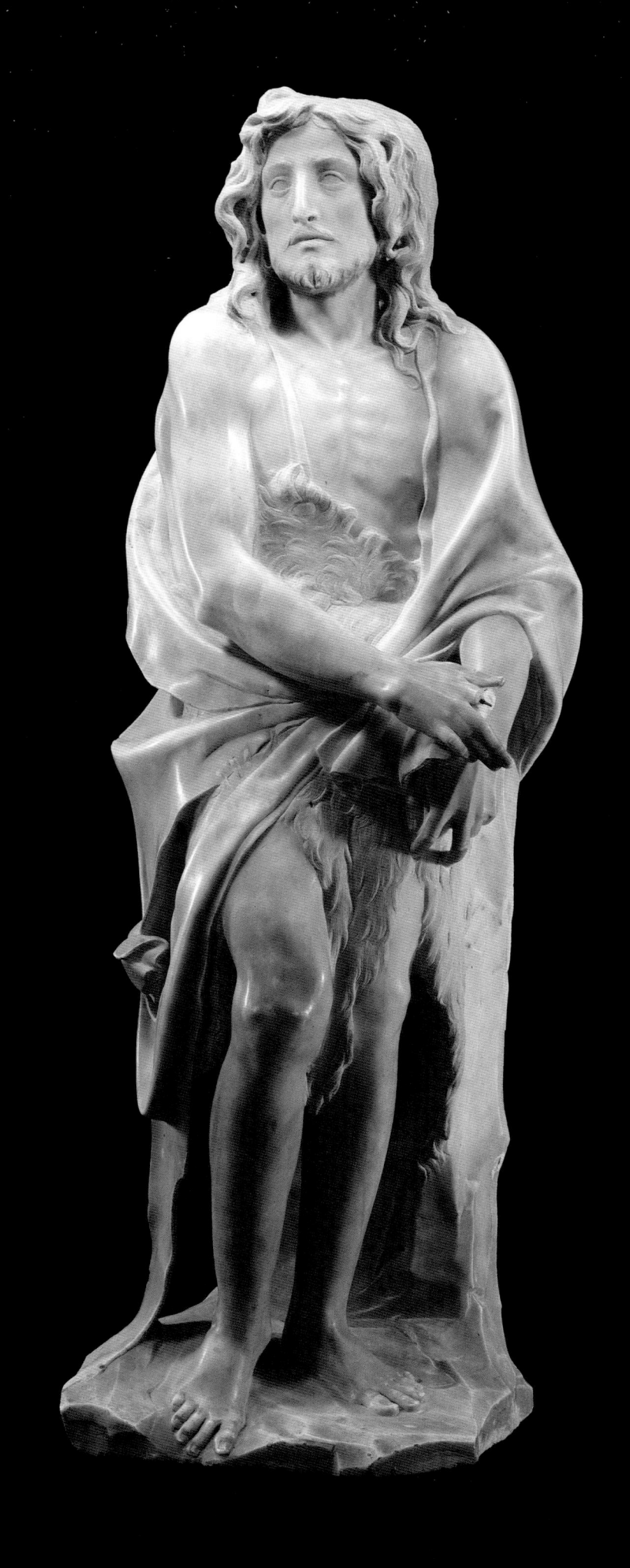

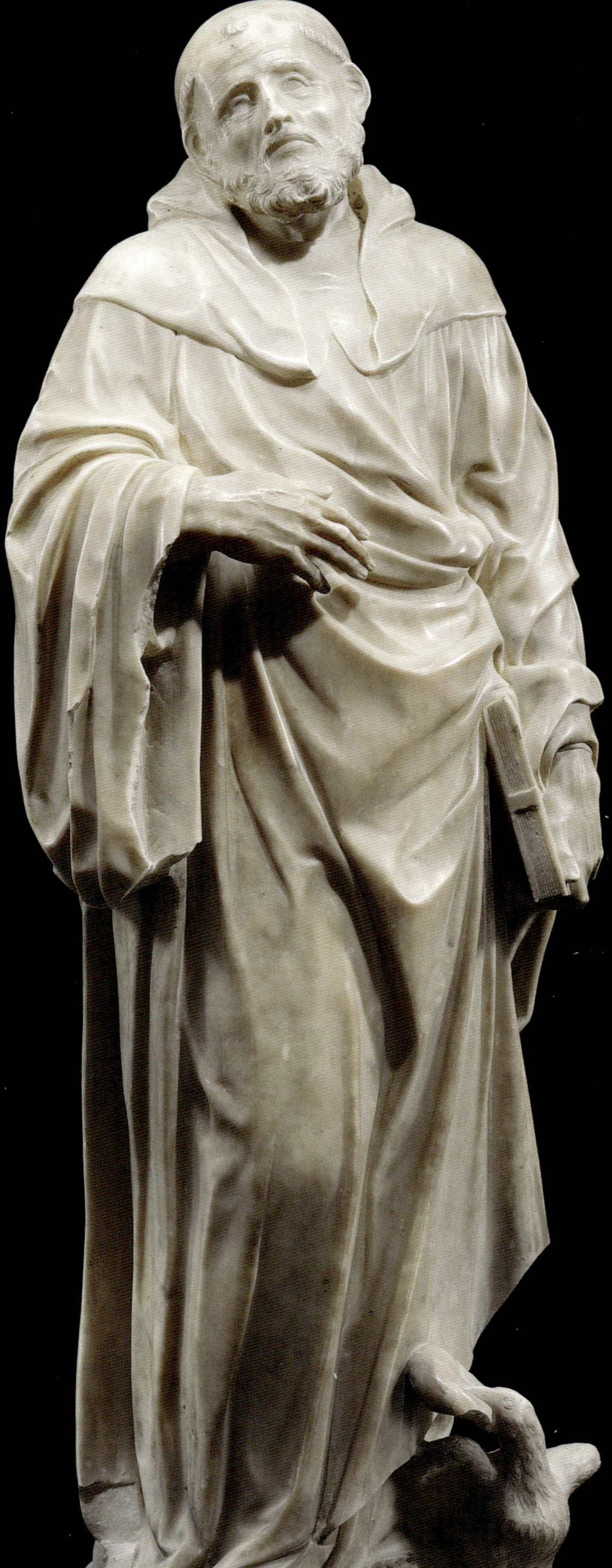

These two magnificent statues in excellent condition, published here for the first time, are for many reasons exceptional examples of Neapolitan art of the Cinquecento. It is extremely rare, first of all, to find evidence of the golden age of marble sculpture in the southern Italian capital outside of the former Kingdom of Naples or of the Iberian Peninsula. Secondly, the quality and style of the two *Saints* point without a doubt to the early work of Girolamo Santacroce, the leader—together with Giovanni Marigliano da Nola (c. 1488–c. 1558)—of the Neapolitan school of sculpture, and one of the most important sculptors in the Italian High Renaissance. Lastly, we are able to identify with certainty the prestigious original location of these two masterpieces.

Their Neapolitan origin is immediately evident in the appearance of the two figures. The young *Baptist*, in his wild but extremely sophisticated physiognomy, descends from the glorious tradition of the Florentine Renaissance (particularly the precedents of Donatello, Benedetto da Maiano, Andrea Sansovino, Giovanfrancesco Rustici, Francesco da Sangallo); but his pose is more peculiar—his hands are placed on his left side to hold a cartouche and a cross (the latter in wood or metal, now lost)—and especially reminiscent of a *Baptist* by Giovanni da Nola in the collection of the Princes of Liechtenstein (Naldi, 1998, *op. cit.*). This statue, however, dates to around 1530, almost a decade later than our *Baptist*, to which it is indebted. In at least two representations of Saint Benedict by Santacroce and Marigliano, furthermore, we find the attribute of the crow holding a piece of bread in its beak—a rare instance in monumental sculpture—alluding to the legend in which the saint was saved by the bird, who snatched the poisoned food away from him. (Santacroce's sculpture, originally in the church of Santa Maria a Cappella Vecchia in Naples, is now in the Seminario Arcivescovile of the same city: Naldi, 1997, *op. cit.*, figs. 210–212; Marigliano's sculpture surmounts the tomb of Jacopo Sanseverino della Saponara in the church of Santi Severino e Sossio in Naples: R. Pane, *Il Rinascimento nell'Italia meridionale*, Milan, 1975–1977, II, fig. 196.)

Santacroce's authorship of the sculpture is defensible not only through the easily recognizable correspondences of type and iconography, but also by its terse, and yet nervous modeling of flesh and drapery, the highly artful display of noble features of the protagonists, and the rather self-conscious craftsmanship (for instance in the *négligée* fur-skin of the penitent, or in his cloak with train, or in the monk's hands). Among the numerous, compelling comparisons with other works by the same artist, the most outstanding is that of the *Baptist* for the altarpiece of the *Epiphany* in the Caracciolo di Vico chapel in San Giovanni a Carbonara in Naples (figs. 1 and 2). Through this marble group, the two Castilian masters Bartolomé Ordoñez and Diego de Siloé, who received this commission around 1515 and executed its main components by around 1517, deeply influenced the fate of sculpture in the former southern kingdom, which had recently become a Spanish viceroyalty. The young Santacroce collaborated in the Caracciolo altarpiece, executing the

fig. 1   *fig. 2*

Baptist for the left-hand niche—stolen in 1977 and as yet unrecovered—and the half figure of the *Evangelist Saint Mark* in the left-hand panel of the predella (Naldi, 1997, *op. cit.*, figs. 1–2, 4, 6).

Possibly born into a family of goldsmiths, Santacroce certainly began his precocious artistic career—a true *enfant prodige*—as a goldsmith. Soon, however, he turned to monumental sculpture, and it is now an accepted and indeed a likely notion to think that this decisive passage was precipitated by his contact after 1515 with Ordoñez and Siloé. Through these masters, who had spent considerable time in Tuscany and in Rome, the young Santacroce was able to expand his knowledge of the Florentine Renaissance beyond an awareness of numerous masterpieces from an earlier period that were visible in Naples (Donatello and Michelozzo, Antonio Rossellino, Benedetto da Maiano, Andrea Ferrucci), and become acquainted with the grandiose Roman styles of Michelangelo, Raphael, Andrea and Jacopo Sansovino. The artist's relationship with the more advanced "modern manner" of Italian art therefore began prior to his visit to Rome and Florence in 1521–1522. But this influence naturally became even more profound after 1522, when Santacroce returned definitively to Naples and established himself as one of the driving forces of the Renaissance, exerting his influence even on Giovanni da Nola (although this artist was his senior), and gaining a respectable place in the *Vite* by Giorgio Vasari (1550, 1568), who was notoriously reluctant to acknowledge southern Italian artists.

Compared with three other representations of John the Baptist by Santacroce (the sculpture of San Giovanni a Carbonara; the high relief for the Altare del Pezzo in Santa Maria di Monteoliveto, later renamed Sant'Anna dei Lombardi [Naldi, 1997, *op. cit.,* figs.

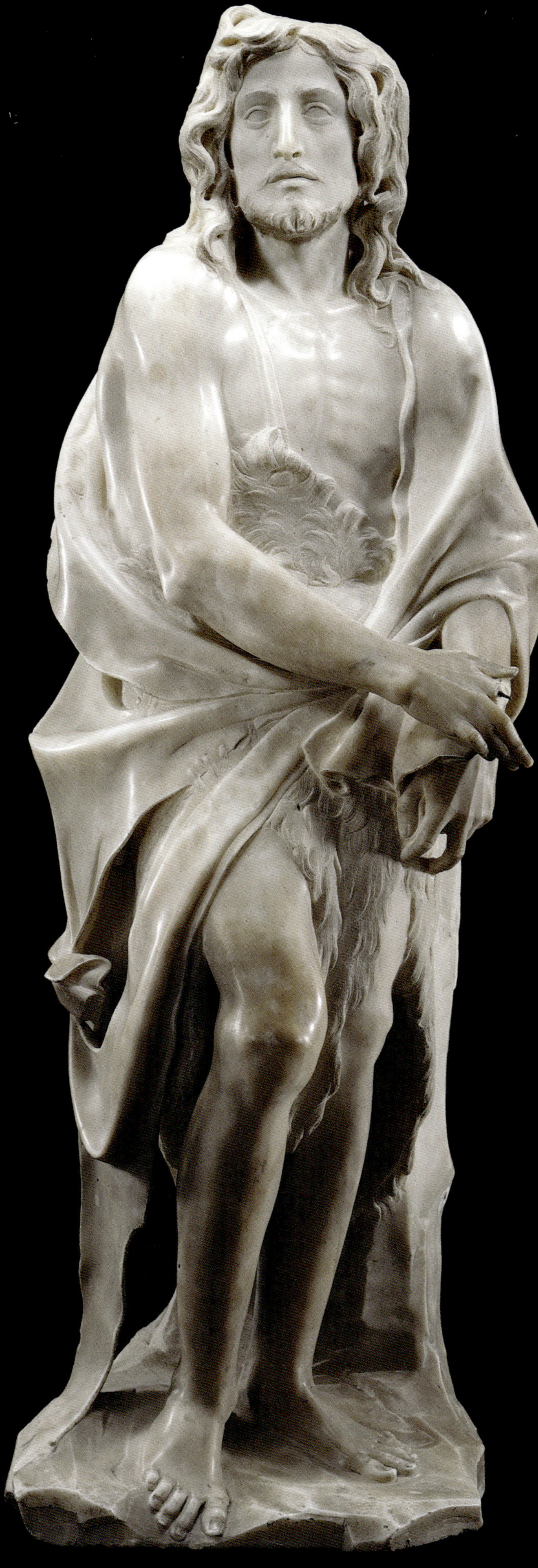

fig. 3

51, 70–71, 77–78]; the sculpture formerly in Santa Maria a Cappella Vecchia, today in the Seminario Arcivescovile of Naples [Naldi, 1997, *op. cit.*, figs. 205–209]), our *Baptist* reveals a more primitive character, closer to the models by Ordoñez, pointing to a dating prior to 1521 for the research—and the discovery—relevant to both this figure and that of *Saint Benedict*.

In the Palazzo Arcivescovile of Capua, in the chapel of Saint Paul, there is today visible a marble altarpiece of superb quality (fig. 3), only recently published in a monograph (Naldi, 1996, *op. cit.*). The organization of this work, which illustrates the Nativity of Christ, is very similar to the Caracciolo altarpiece. But even more important and direct models for it were the two brilliant Florentine sculptures that, visible in Naples from the late Quattrocento in the church of Santa Maria di Monteoliveto, had inspired the Caracciolo altarpiece itself: the Piccolomini d'Aragona Altar, a work representing the Nativity by Antonio Rossellino (1471–1474), and the Correale di Terranova Altar by Benedetto da Maiano, depicting the Annunciation (1489–1491). A large rectangular relief featuring the the evangelic scene constituted—and still constitutes—the central panel of the triptych, subdivided by four small pilasters. On the sides of the central panel were two niches made of red marble containing two sculptures of *Saints*. The niches were surmounted by two *oculi* out from which peeked two half-figures of *Prophets*. This composition rested on a predella in the shape of a stylobate, almost like the façade of a miniature temple; similarly, the pediment for the entire frontispiece was articulated by a classical entablature (architrave, frieze, cornice). The altarpiece's current location and its appearance are not original, as is revealed by several incongruous elements of reassemblage: the frieze and the predella are

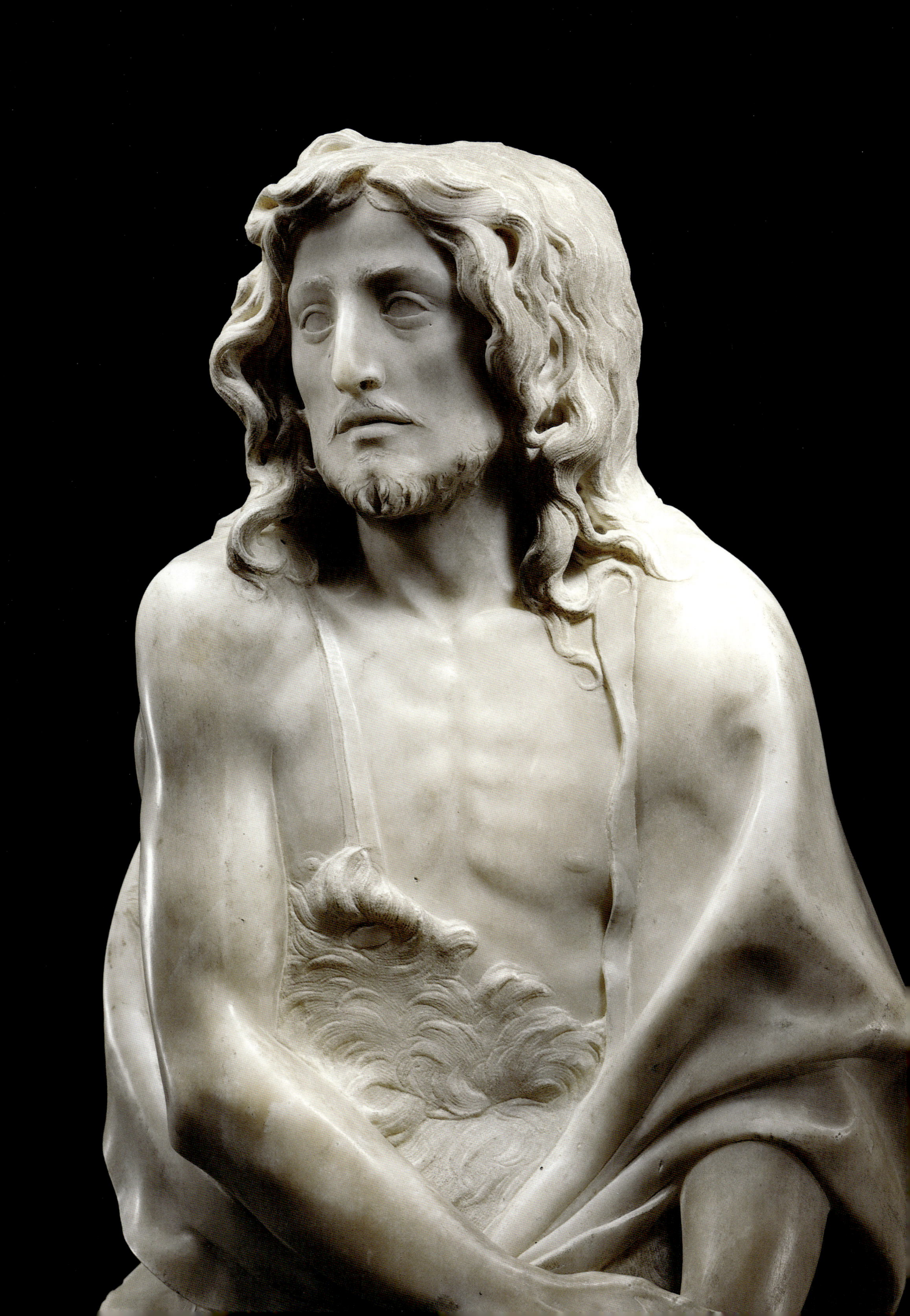

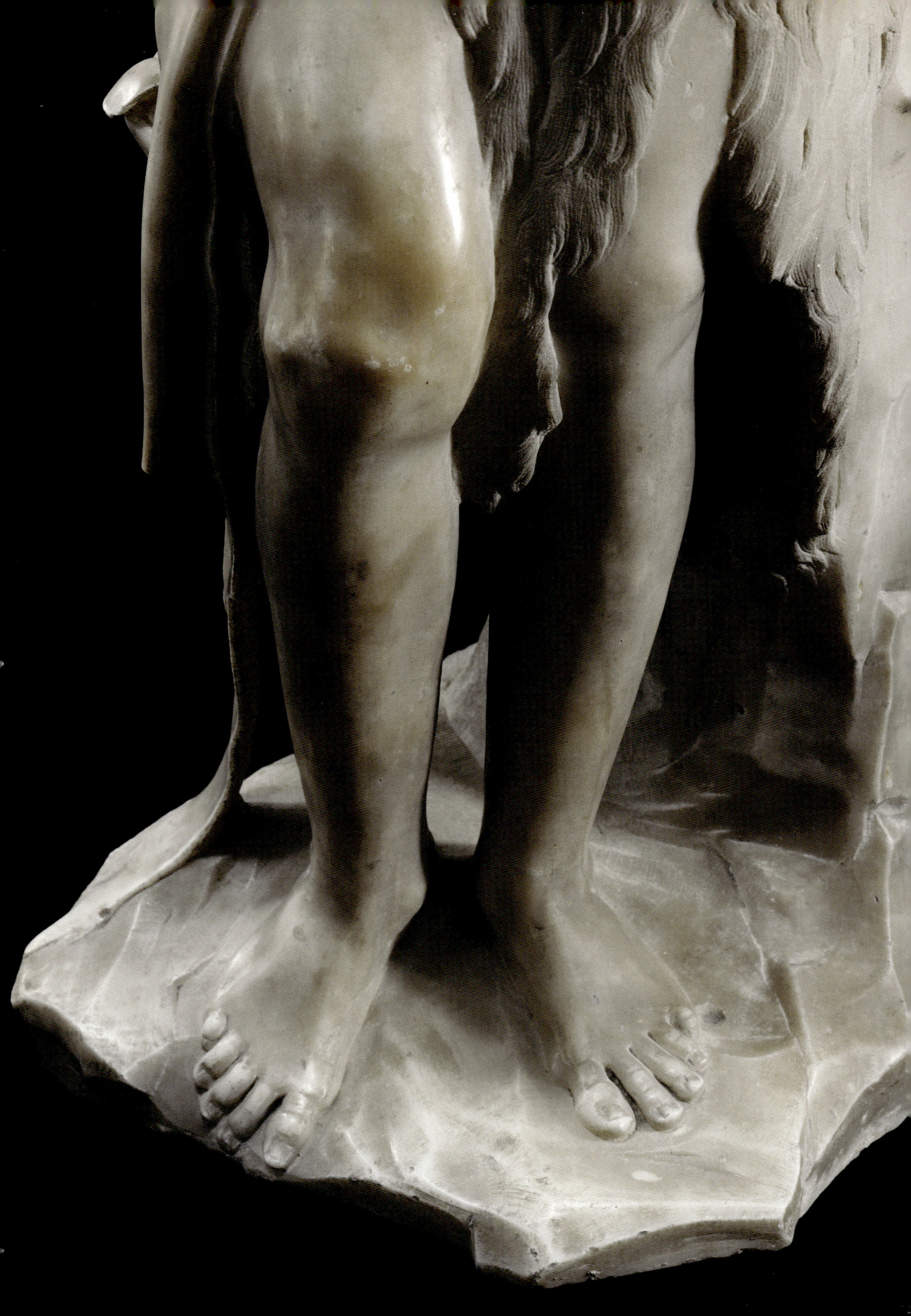

not made of Carrara marble, but of a mixed stone from Campania; the two *oculi* between the capitals of the small pilasters are lost, replaced by two terracotta metopes with festoons; the two half-figures of the *Prophets,* which were originally in the *oculi* are now in the niches, each improperly located above a high double plinth (a cube of mixed stone, and, in the middle section, a molded element in the shape of a *prie-dieu*). The width of each niche has been reduced from both sides, and the conch has been elevated to a higher level, just below the capitals, whereas in the two altars of Monteoliveto, where the *oculi* survive, the conchs are found at a lower level. The tampering with the *oculi* and the niches was clearly intended to compensate for the disappearance of two statues that measured at least 90 cm. and at most 95 cm. in height, as the panel of the *Nativity* is 147.5 cm. tall, and the two *Prophets* are 30 cm. tall on the left, and 33 cm. on the right (for details see Naldi, 1996, *op. cit.*).

A recent re-examination of the existing bibliography, together with new documentary evidence, explains the reasons for these incongruities, also revealing with certainty the original location of the *Nativity* altarpiece. This work was originally for the high altar of the church—first Benedictine, then Jesuit—of San Benedetto in Capua (now dedicated to the Immaculate Conception), and came to be installed in the bishop's palace by order of archbishop Baldassarre Mormile in 1819. This important church suffered very serious architectural and artistic damage during the French occupation (1806–1815), when it had been deconsecrated and adapted for a variety of inappropriate purposes. Under these circumstances the frieze and the predella were lost, together with the two lateral statues that represented *Saint John the Baptist* (on the left), and *Saint Benedict* (on the right). The selection of these two characters can be accounted for by the wish to honor the titular saint of the church and the eponymous saint of the patron of the altar, Giovan Battista de Angelis, abbot of San Benedetto during the first quarter of the sixteenth century (for all relevant information see Amirante, *op. cit.*, especially pp. 102–114 n. 5 and notes 53–82, Appendix n. 5; and Chillemi, *op. cit.*).

Our sculptures correspond precisely to the two missing pieces from Capua, not only in terms of type, iconography and size, but also in style and chronology. We know that Giovan Battista de Angelis, a rich and ambitious Neapolitan patron, after spending about twenty years at the ancient monastery of San Benedetto in the role of commendatory abbot from the beginning of the century, obtained a bull on 13 May 1519 from Pope Leo X de'Medici whereby San Benedetto, no longer inhabited by monks, was transformed into a collegiate church of twelve canons, under the patronage of the de Angelis family, who for several generations had supplied the abbots for the monastery (Orsini, *op. cit.*; Ruotolo, *op. cit.*). Immediately after the enactment of the papal bull, Giovan Battista, by then rector of the collegiate church with the title of secular abbot, resumed the vast decoration work for the church that had been in progress at least since 1501, and focused initially on the high altar (Amirante, *op. cit.*).

The Capua *Nativity* and the *Prophets* are certainly not by Santacroce. But the *Prophets* have been convincingly attributed to Giovan Giacomo da Brescia (Naldi, 1996, *op. cit.*), another important Neapolitan sculptor (though originally from Lombardy), documented between Naples and Carrara from 1519 to 1525, usually in collaboration with Santacroce. The *Nativity* has been attributed to an anonymous, though close, assistant of Ordoñez (Naldi, 1996, *op. cit.*), the sculptor directly linked to Santacroce's training and early work. The data therefore suggest that, for the sake of expediency, the dynamic de Angelis entrusted the Capua altarpiece to three different artists, who were nevertheless associated with one another by their previous relationship with Ordoñez. It is possible that the patron originally wished to commission the works from Ordoñez himself, in view of the recent success of the Altare Caracciolo di Vico. However, in the spring of 1519, when the abbot of San Benedetto finally obtained the bull from Leo X and was therefore able to assume patronage of the high altar, Ordoñez had already left Naples, travelling between Spain and Carrara to execute some major works destined for his country (including the tomb of the Catholic Kings, parents of Emperor Charles V, in Granada). In December 1520 Ordoñez died suddenly in Carrara, leaving the Spanish monuments unfinished: in 1521 Santacroce and Giovan Giacomo da Brescia arrived together from Naples, two among the sculptors called to replace Ordoñez in the Apuan quarries; the two artists remained in Tuscany at least during 1522 (see esp. Naldi, 1997, *op. cit.*).

In view of this evidence, the execution of the Capua altarpiece can be securely placed between the spring of 1519 and the autumn of 1520. The *Baptist* and *Saint Benedict* are therefore the first sculptures by Santacroce that can be dated with certainty; they lead us to wonder whether the Caracciolo di Vico *Baptist*, sometimes believed to be the earliest work in marble by the young master (c. 1516), should in fact be considered a later work, dating no earlier than 1520–1521, or even c. 1523.

Francesco Caglioti

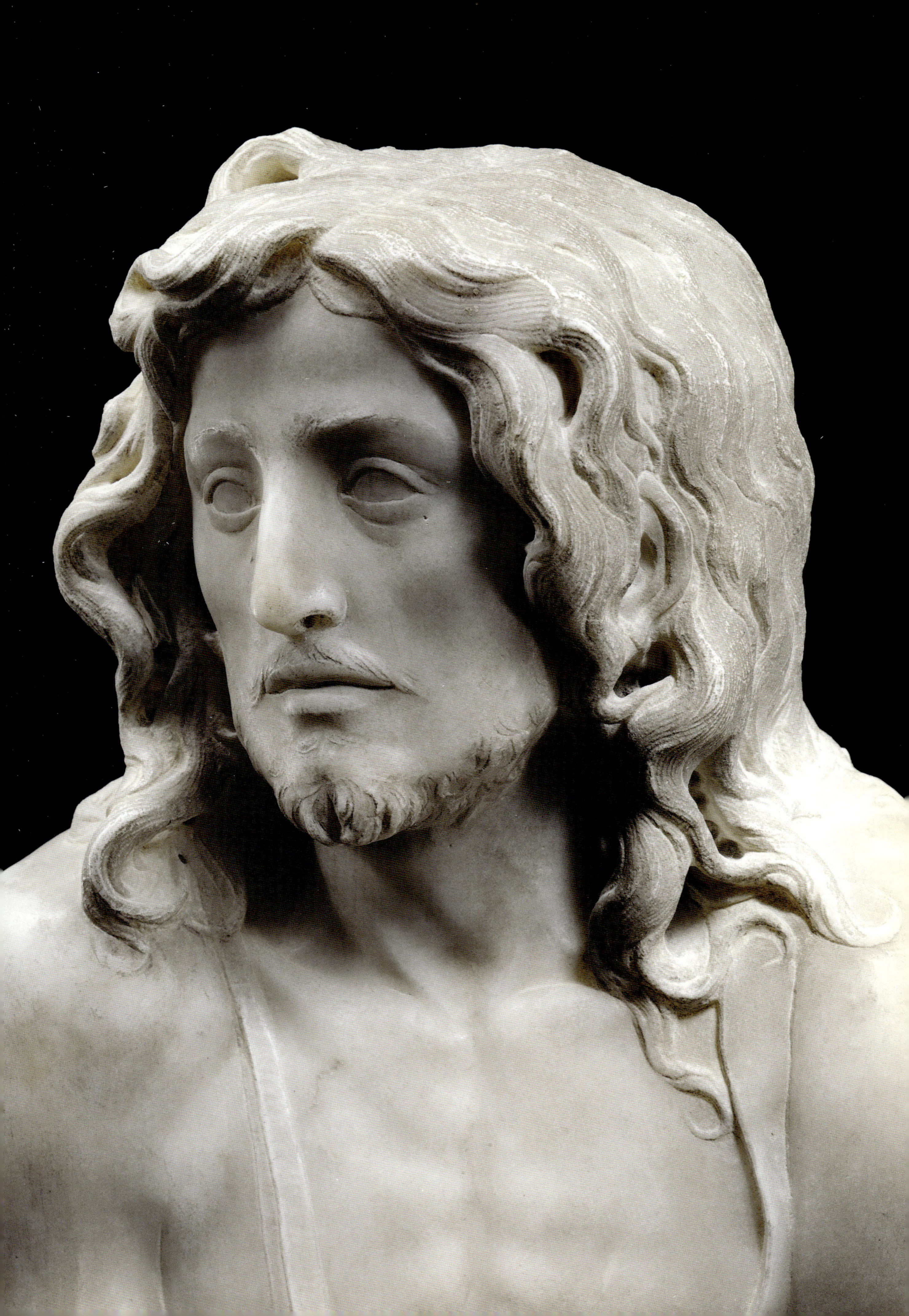

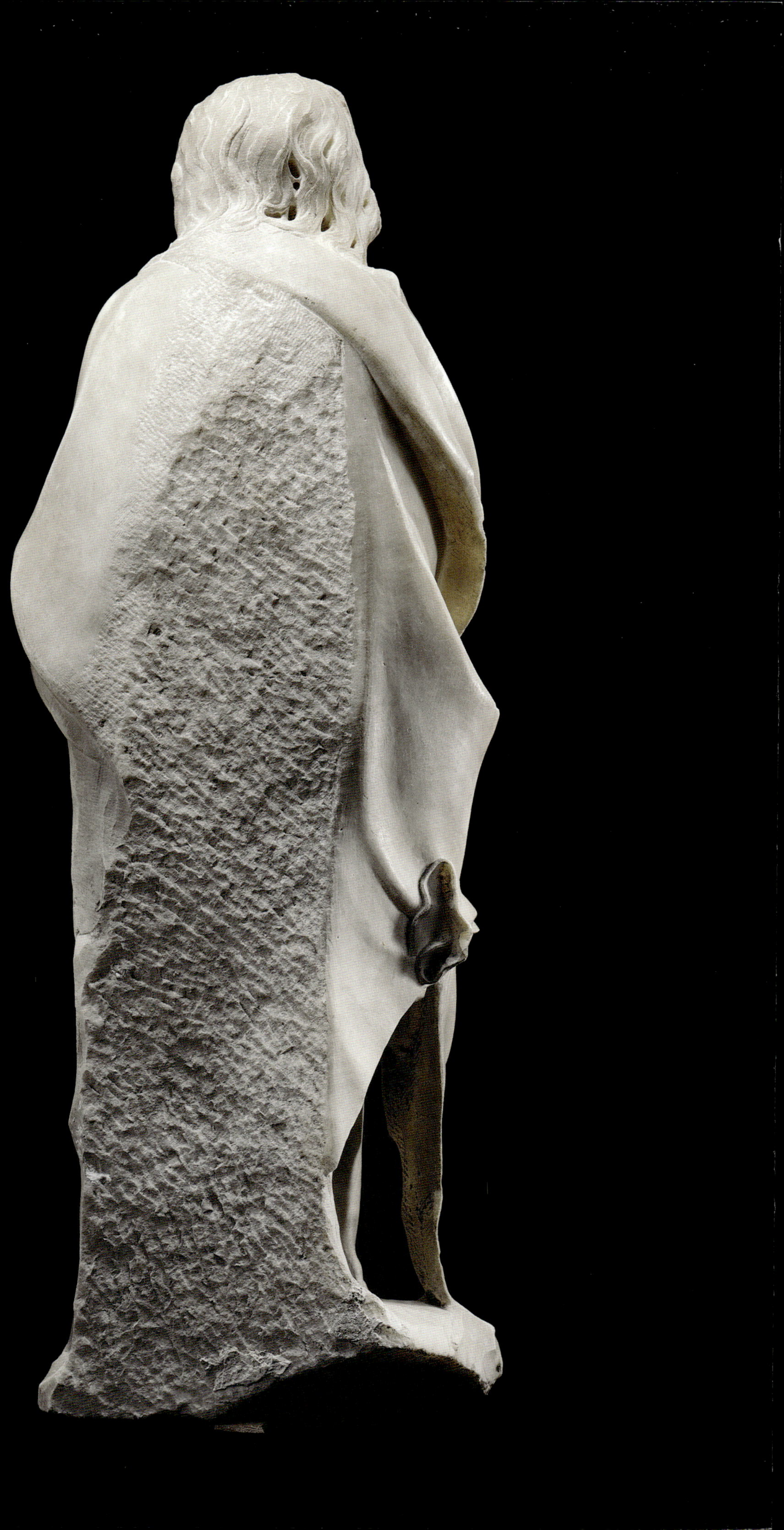

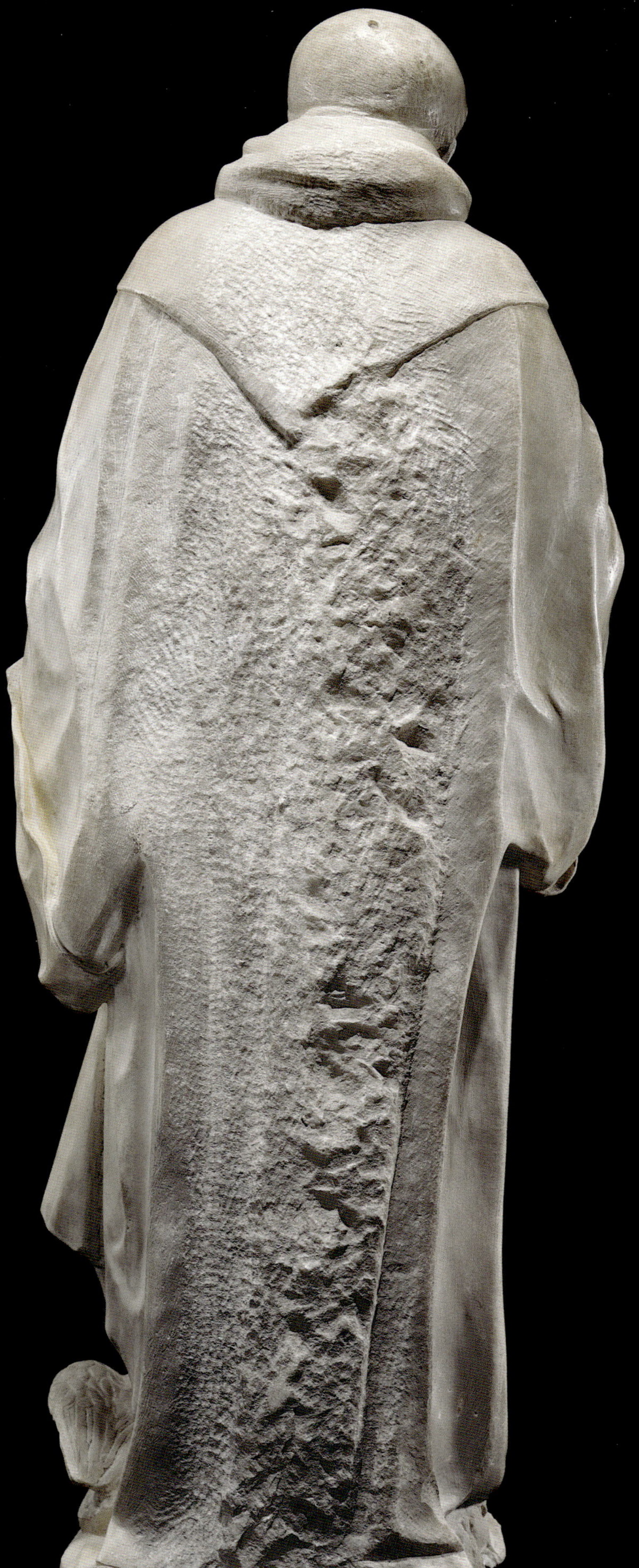

MAFFEO OLIVIERI
(Brescia 1484–1543/44)

Candelabrum

Bronze, on marble and porphyry base
33 cm. (13 in.) high, including base
c. 1527

Provenance:

Private Collection, Sweden
Private Collection, USA

Exhibited:

National Gallery of Art, Washington, D.C., November–
    December 1998
Philadelphia Museum of Art, 1999–2003

Relevant Bibliography:

W. Bode, *Die italienische Bronzestatuetten der Renaissance,* Vienna, 1906

___, "Maffeo Olivieri," *Jahrbuch der Königlich Preussischen Kunstsammlungen,* Vol. XXX, 1909, pp. 81–88

L. Planiscig, *Venezianische Bildhauer der Renaissance,* Vienna, 1921, pp. 306–308

___, *Piccoli bronzi italiani del Rinascimento,* Milan, 1930, pp. 27–28

___, "Maffeo Olivieri," *Dedalo,* Vol. XII, 1932, pp. 34–35

A. Morassi, "Per la ricostruzione di Maffeo Olivieri," *Bollettino d'Arte,* III, 1936, pp. 237–249

F. Rossi, "Maffeo Olivieri e la bronzistica bresciana del '500," *Arte Lombarda,* 47–48, 1977, pp. 115–134

L. Zendri, "L'attività di uno scultore bresciano nella prima metà del Cinquecento: Maffeo Olivieri (1484–1542/43) 'intayatore lignaminum' e bronzista," Ph. D. diss., Università degli Studi di Trento, 2002/2003

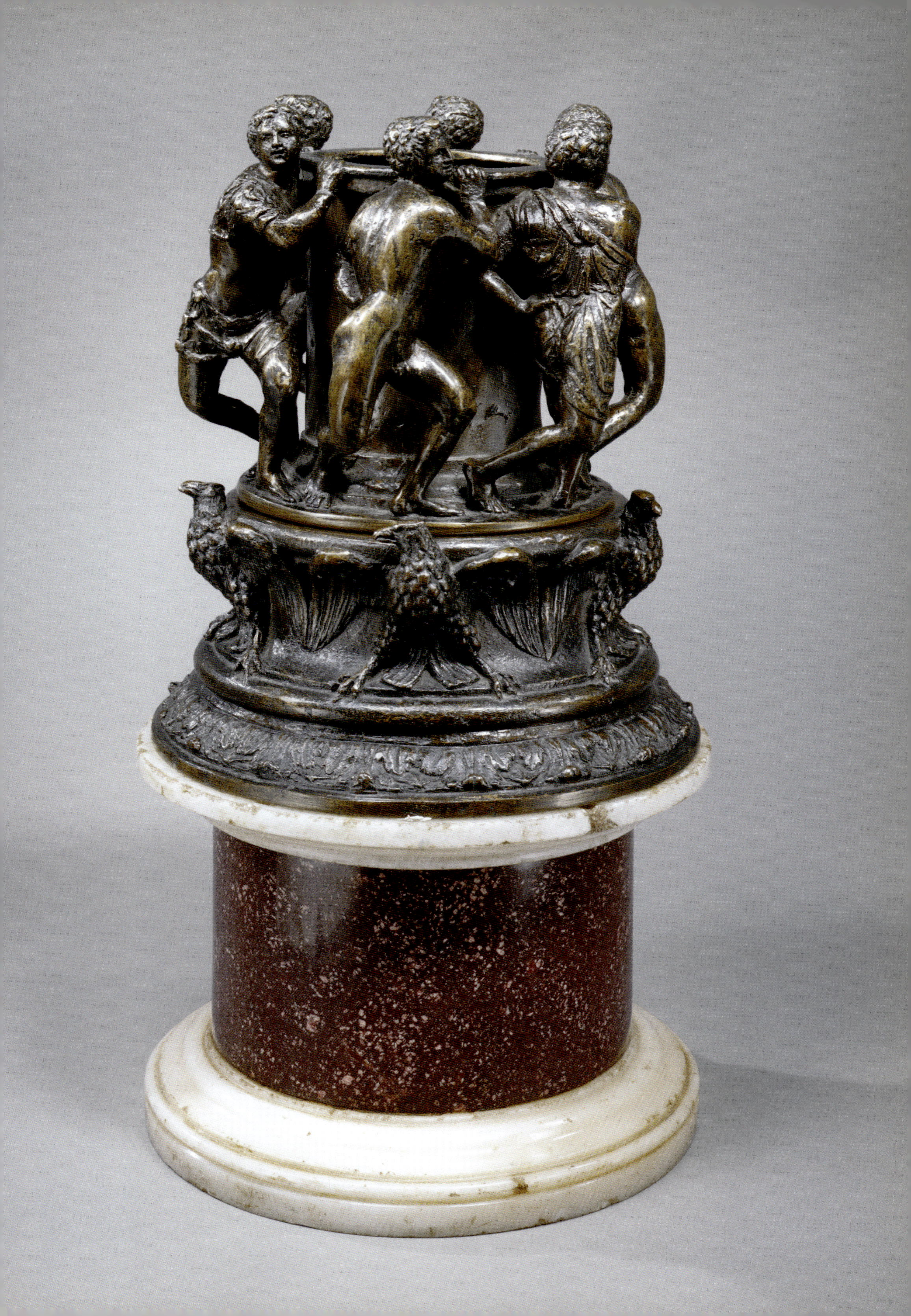

fig. 1

fig. 2

fig. 3

fig. 4

Maffeo Olivieri was an important sculptor, medallist and wood-carver in Venice, the Veneto and Trentino at the beginning of the sixteenth century. There are many surviving works by this artist in wood, most notably perhaps, the crucifix of Sarezzo (Brescia), and the large altarpiece of the Assumption of the Virgin in Condino (Trento), both commissioned in 1538. The Martinengo Monument in Brescia is also often thought to be by him. Certainly his most celebrated sculptures are the pair of bronze candelabra that he made for the Sacrament Chapel of San Marco, Venice (fig. 1). Commissioned by the highly distinguished patron, Altobello Averoldi (c. 1465–1531), the two candelabra were donated on Christmas Eve, 1527. Each of the candelabra stands 1.89 meters in height and is decorated with eight tiers of decorative motifs that are secular or classical in style, and yet, surely, rich in coded or enigmatic religious symbolism. No doubt the chief model for these candelabra was the Paschal Candlestick by Riccio at the Santo in Padua, where the same disjunction between style and content is apparent.

The present sculpture is closely associated with the San Marco candelabra. Our piece is composed of two sections that were modeled and cast separately and then artfully chased and assembled. In the lower section, five eagles, facing frontally, encircle the shaft of the candelabrum. In the upper section, six male youths, three nude and three dressed *all'antica*, dance or run around the candelabrum. These motifs are nearly identical to motifs on the San Marco candelabra. At San Marco, there is a band of similar eagles in the third tier of decoration on the candelabra (fig. 2); and a circle of comparable running figures occupies the seventh tier of the candelabra (figs. 3 and 4).

Despite such similarities, the present work differs from the pieces at San Marco in several significant ways. First, on the present work, the lower rim of the bottom section is terminated with a molding ornamented with a leaf decoration. This is not true at San Marco, and this molding does not seem to appear anywhere else on the candelabra. Second, on the present work, there are five eagles. At San Marco, it appears that there are only four eagles on each of the candelabra (fig. 2). Furthermore, the chasing and patination differ. The present piece is more finely worked in some details. And, significantly, the present piece has extensive traces of gilding in the interstices of the wings of the eagles, indicating that the eagles were once completely gilded. It is also possible, although as yet uncertain, that the entire base was gilded; if so, one would have to imagine the complete piece covered in gold leaf. By contrast, there is no gilding evident on the San Marco candelabra, which are covered with the black patination typical of early sixteenth-century Venetian bronzes.

One should note, furthermore, that there is no indication that the present piece is incomplete. On the contrary, the lack of wear to the surface and edges of the upper section suggest that it never had another section resting on top of it.

Given these differences, order of precedence cannot be established with certainty; it cannot be shown whether the present work or the San Marco candelabra came first. The

fig. 5

present work might be a trial piece that was made in preparation for casting the candelabra, and subsequently gilded; or it might be a completely independent work, a variant on a smaller scale.

The patron of the San Marco candelabra was Altobello Averoldi, who was the Bishop of Pola and the Papal Legate to Venice. Although a member of the Brescian nobility, he was raised in the Roman court of Cardinal Raffaele Riario. Like Riario, Altobello Averoldi was one of the most demanding and sophisticated patrons of the early Cinquecento; he was portrayed by the Bolognese painter Francesco Francia in a panel now at the National Gallery of Art in Washington (fig. 5), and in 1520–1522 commissioned from Titian a spectacular altarpiece for the church of Santi Nazaro e Celso in Brescia. An exceptionally discerning art connoisseur, it is significant that Averoldi selected Olivieri to make the candelabra. Although the inscriptions on the candelabra at San Marco point out Brescia as the place of origin both of the artist and the patron, it was not mere civic pride that dictated the choice of the artist. Brescia enjoyed a long tradition of bronze sculpture; presumably, Averoldi could have hired another Brescian sculptor or bronze caster, such as the Master of 1523, Antonio da Brescia, or Fra Giulio da Brescia, all of whom were active in the 1520s. What is more, the close resemblance between the San Marco candelabra and the bronze piece examined here leads us to think that perhaps this too was commissioned by Averoldi, possibly for his private collection, precisely as a reminder of this important donation.

Maffeo Olivieri's artistic significance in the history of sculpture from the Veneto during the period between Riccio and Sansovino was recognized by Leo Planiscig. Olivieri's

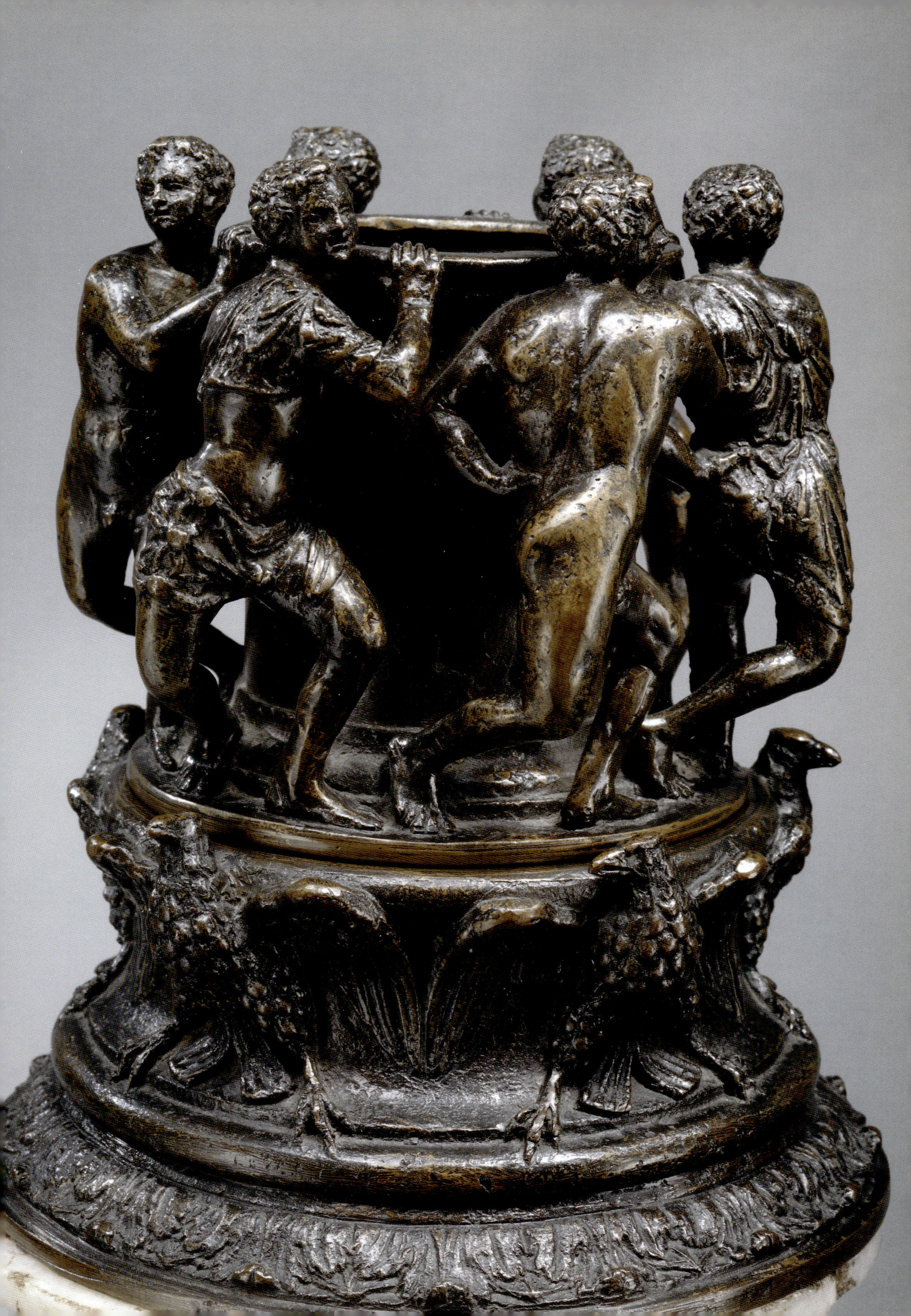

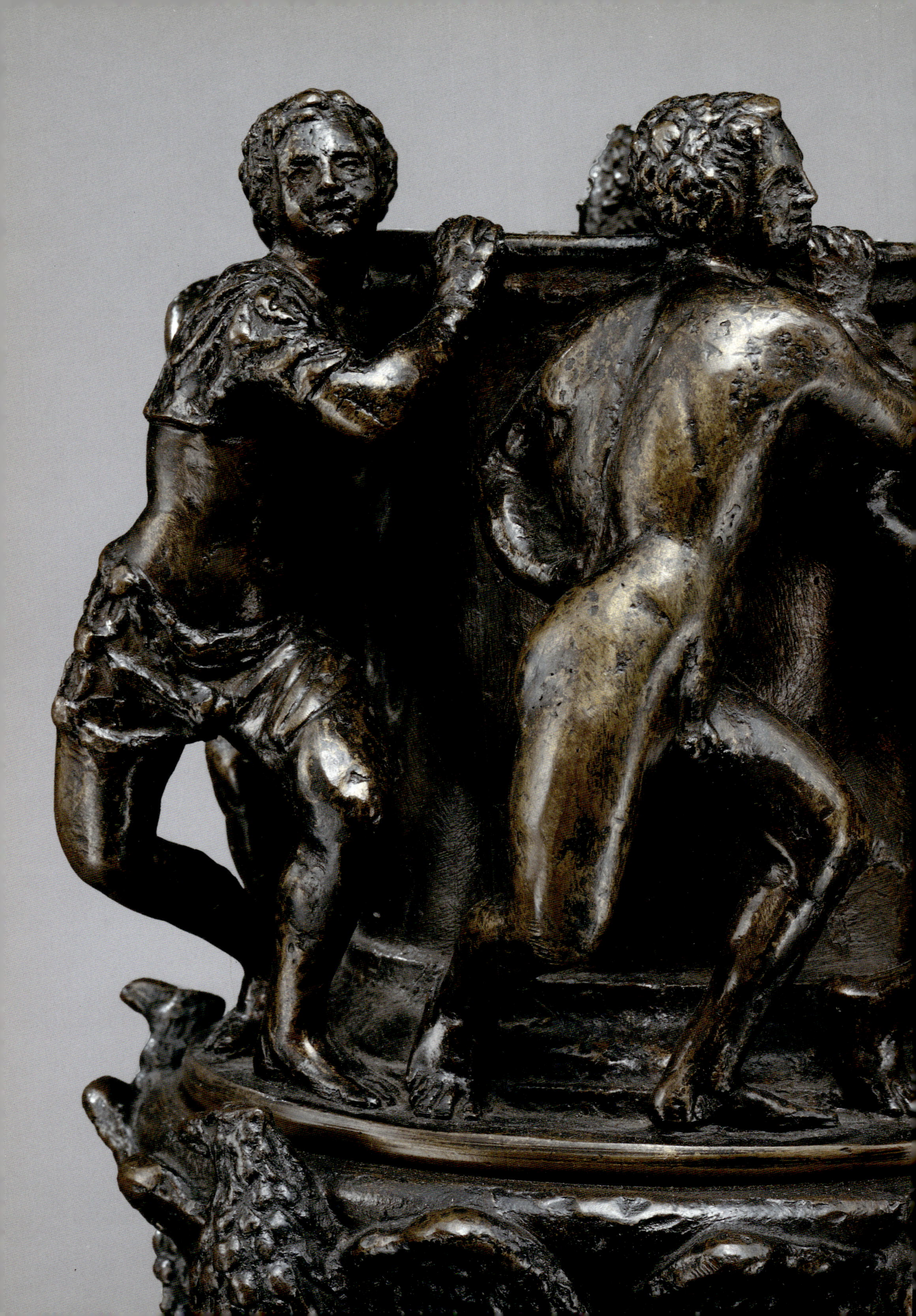

wood sculptures, with their strong features and "popular" character, adhere perfectly to the Lombard style, typified by the robust realism of Vincenzo Foppa's paintings and the lively expressionism of Stefano Lamberti's sculpture. His bronze production, however, reveals a different stylistic approach, characterized by constant references to the antique, and influenced by the sculpture traditions of the Veneto and Padua, particularly of Andrea Briosco known as "il Riccio." The San Marco candelabra are closely comparable to the monumental Paschal Candlestick executed by Riccio between 1507 and 1516 for the Basilica del Santo in Padua. Maffeo, after all, must have shared Riccio's passion for classical sculpture, as is revealed, for example, by the two wax models for the Laocoön mentioned in the inventory of his workshop in Brescia. Olivieri must have carefully studied the elaborate structure of Riccio's candlestick, and it is interesting to recognize the originality of his variations on the motifs from the Paduan bronze. In particular the six running figures, which also feature in the present work, represent a brilliant and original reworking of the bacchanalia of putti executed by Riccio, still closely reminiscent of Donatello's example. It is not surprising, therefore, that when he was asked to execute a candelabrum, probably destined for a private collection, Maffeo used this same motif of the San Marco candelabra. But if Olivieri's taste for the antique was indebted to the sculpture of Riccio, nevertheless the Venetian candelabra reveal a sharper realism, clearly linked to Lombard tradition, and comparable instead to the paintings of Romanino.

In spite of the certain attribution of the candelabra in the Sacrament Chapel of San Marco, a catalogue of Maffeo Olivieri's work in bronze remains to be written. Scholars (Bode, 1906, 1909, *op. cit.*; Planiscig 1921, 1930, 1932, *op. cit.*; Morassi, *op. cit.*; Rossi, *op. cit.*) have tentatively attributed to Olivieri several small bronze works in which they have noticed similarities to the figures of the Virtues and of the naked youths of the San Marco candelabra. (The most interesting among these are *Adam with the Spade* formerly in Berlin, and *Venus Lashing Cupid* in the Getty Museum.) However, these attributions are not supported by documentary evidence and are also indefensible in terms of style. This reinforces the importance of the present bronze, the only work that can be convincingly associated with the candelabra in San Marco, and therefore attributed with absolute certainty to Olivieri.

Andrew Butterfield

We are grateful to Laura Zendri for her assistance in the preparation of this catalogue entry.

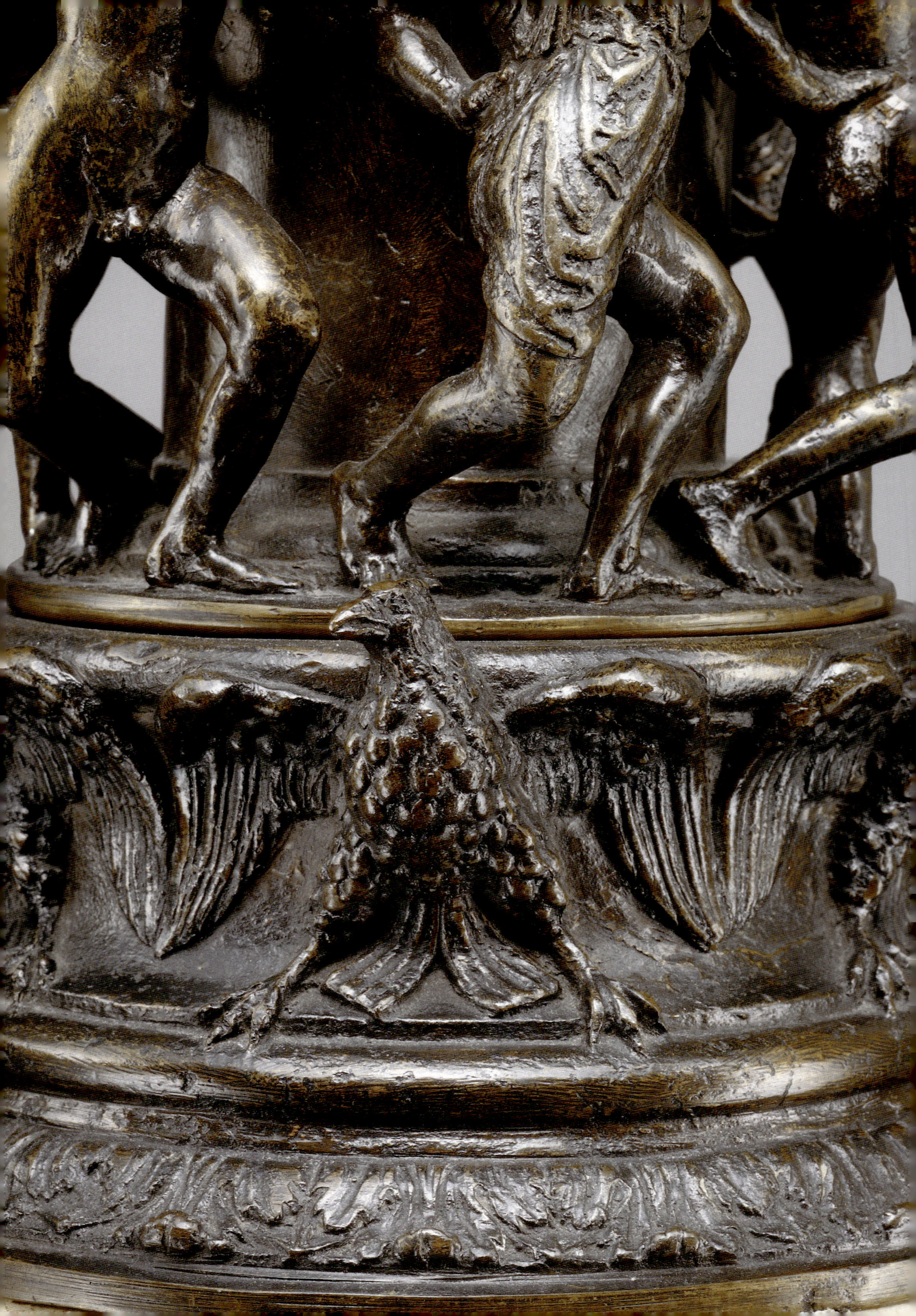

FERDINANDO TACCA
(1619–1686)

Diana and Pan

Bronze
35.5 x 40 cm. (13¾ x 15¾ in.)
Mid-17th century
Inscribed (on a fictive scroll at the base of the rock beneath Diana's left knee): PANE E DIANA; with the French Crown inventory number (on the back of the rock): no. 282

Provenance:

King Louis XIV of France
French Royal collection (until 1796)
Pierre Van Recum (1796–1797)
E. Schellander, Antwerp (1961)
Sale, Christie's London, 3 July 1990, no. 83
Private collection

Exhibited:

Art Institute of Chicago, February 1994–April 2004

Bibliography:

M.J. Guiffrey, "Testament et inventaire après décès de André le Nostre et autres documents le concernant," *Bulletin de la Société de l'Histoire de l'Art Francais*, 1911, p. 224

Inventaire des Tableaux du Garde-Meuble de la Couronne, 1792 (French Archival No. 01 3334) and 1791, p. 148 (copies in the Wallace Collection, London)

Les bronzes de la Couronne (exh. cat., Musée du Louvre, Paris, 12 April–12 July 1999), Paris, 1999, p. 163, no. 282

C. Avery, *Jean Bologne: La Belle endormie* (exh. cat., Galerie Piltzer, Paris, 27 April–6 June 2000), Paris, 2000, pp. 28–29, 53–54, figs. 40, 42

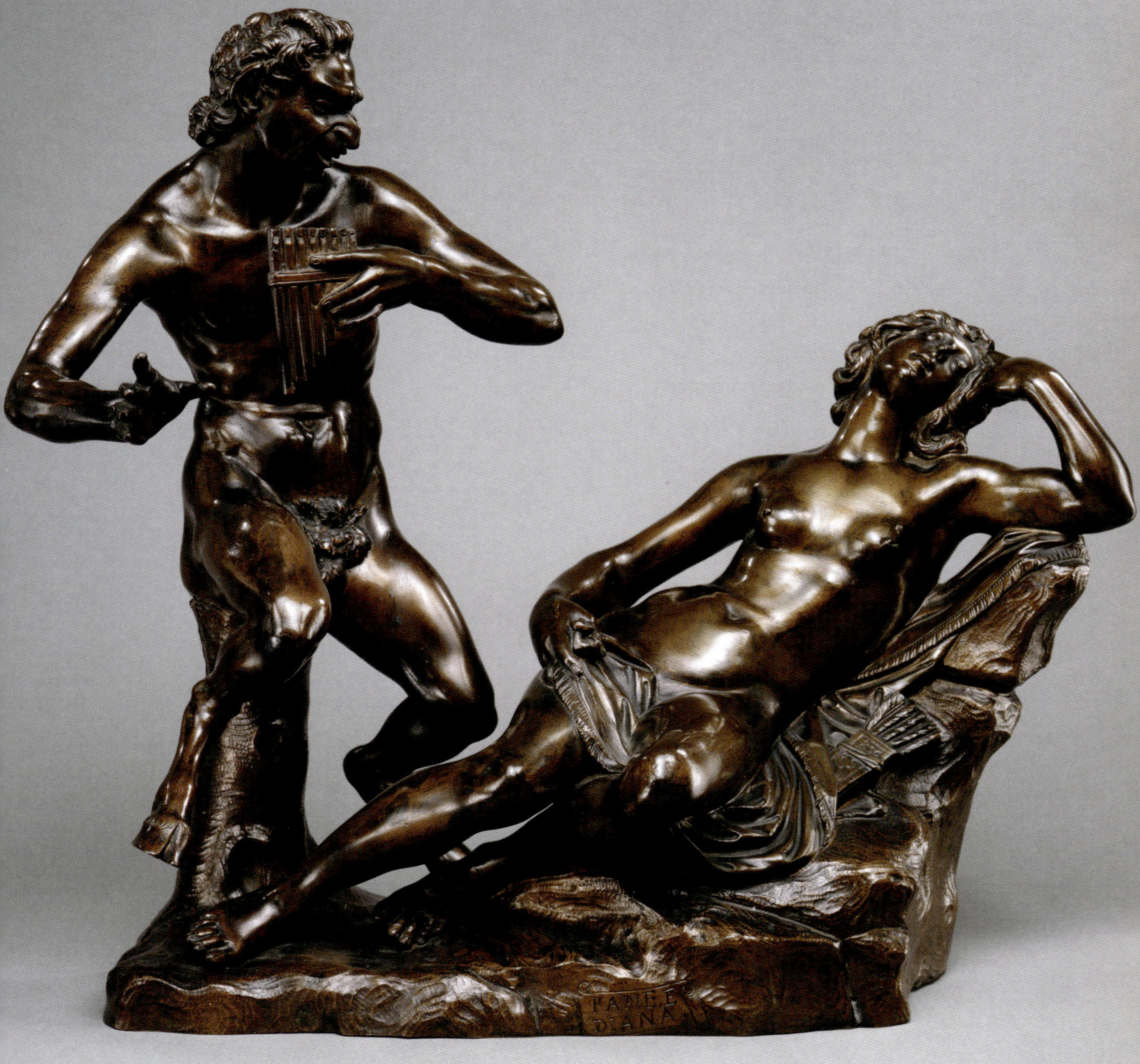
PAN E
DIANA

Relevant Bibliography:

H. Landais, "Sur quelques statuettes légués par le Nôtre à Louis XIV et conservées au Département des objets d'art," *Bulletin des Musées de France*, XIV, 1949, no. 3, pp. 60–63

A. Radcliffe, "Ferdinando Tacca, the Missing Link in Florentine Baroque Bronzes," *Kunst des Barock in der Toskana*, Munich, 1976, pp. 14–23

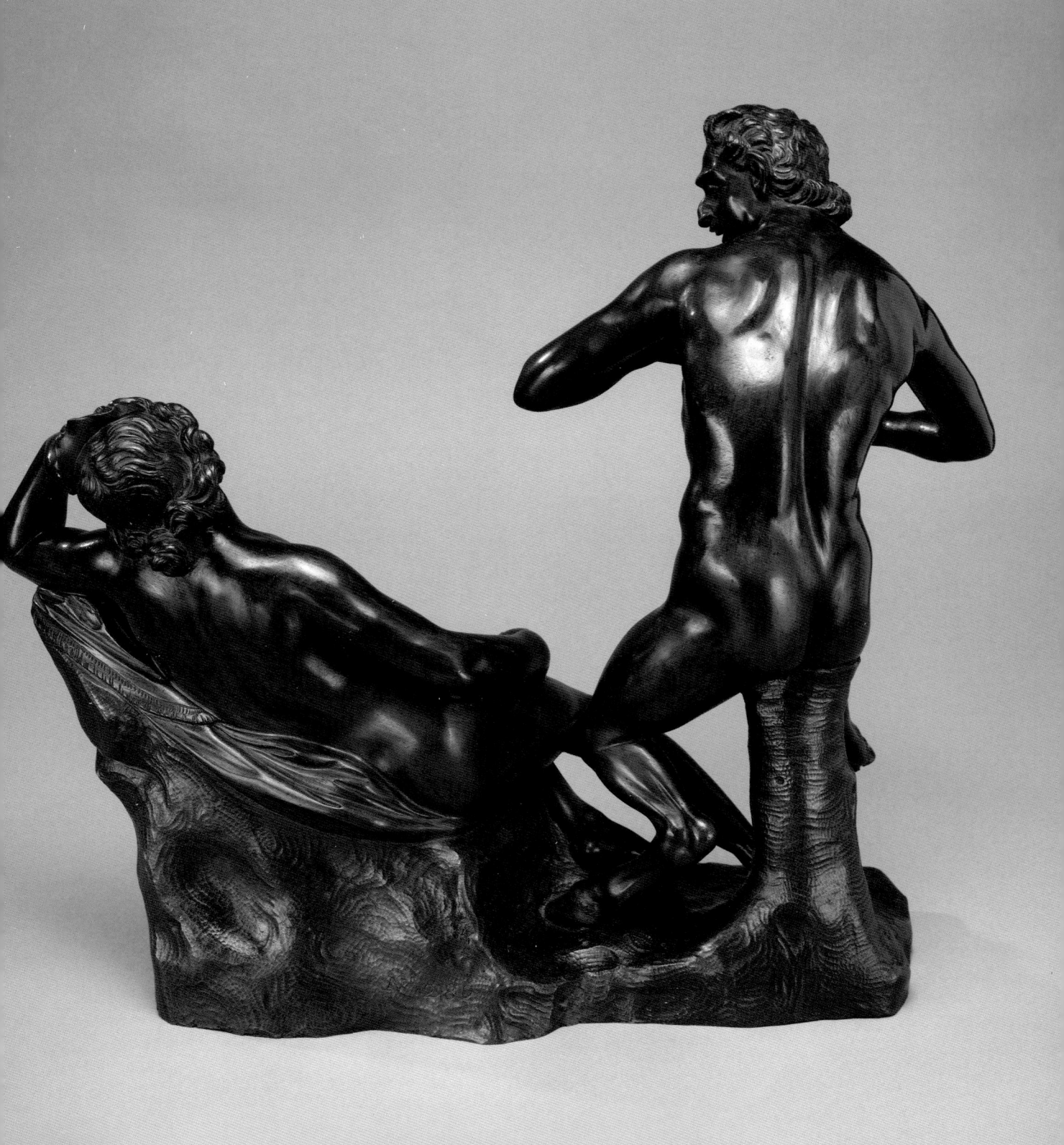

This group of *Diana and Pan* belonged to King Louis XIV of France. It appears as no. 282 in the French Crown inventories of 1707, 1722, 1733, 1776, 1785–1786, 1788, and in 1791, where it is listed as: "Un groupe de Diane nue et en repos, regardée par le Dieu Pan assis sur on tronc d'arbre, haut de treize pouces, bon moderne, estimé quartre cents livres."

Previously, the bronze may have belonged to André le Nôtre, the distinguished art collector and designer of the gardens of Vaux-le-Vicomte and Versailles, who donated many treasures from his collection to Louis XIV in 1693. The sculpture appears to be identifiable with the bronze statuette listed in André le Nôtre's collection as "un de *Diane et un Satire*" (Guiffrey, *op. cit.*, p. 224). Guiffrey noted that the margin of the inventory at this point contained the notation "Neuf de Soussin." Guiffrey speculated that this was a *lapsus* for Poussin, and that this group of bronzes had originally belonged to the great French painter. However, Landais (*op. cit.*) plausibly suggested that the correct interpretation of the name in the margin was Susini, the sculptor and caster associated with Giambologna.

As the authors of the catalogue of the exhibition of *Les bronzes de la Couronne* noted, it is also possible that the bronze may in fact have entered the Royal Collection in 1689 as part of the legacy of Charles Errard, the Director of the French Academy in Rome. This hypothesis is based on the fact that the inventory of Errard's collection mentions a bronze of a "*Femme avec un satyre*" (*Les bronzes de la Couronne, op. cit.*, p. 24, nn. 19 and 25.)

Despite the marginalia in le Nôtre's inventory, it has been widely recognized that the bronze is indeed by Ferdinando Tacca. The son of Pietro Tacca, Ferdinando was the sculptor and architect to the Grand Dukes of Tuscany from 1640 until his death in 1686. In addition, he also worked for the Royal Family of Spain. Among his major projects are the *Equestrian Monument of Philip IV of Spain* in Madrid, the statue of *Ferdinando I de' Medici*, in the Cappella dei Principi, San Lorenzo, Florence, and four bronze *Angels* for the Palazzo Ducale at Massa (two of which are today in the Wallace Collection, London).

The present group is characteristic of Tacca's work (see, for example, fig. 1, Ferdinando Tacca, *Roger and Angelica,* Musée du Louvre, Paris). As Anthony Radcliffe has noted, Tacca transformed the bronze statuette group, concentrating on two figure groups, arranged laterally, and presented in a dramatic or theatrical format:

> "It is my contention that it was Ferdinando Tacca who led the way in Florence towards a new function for the small bronze group, who transformed it from an object to be handled or walked around into a sort of miniature theatre to be precisely placed upon a piece of furniture. . . . Perhaps it is not after all irrelevant that he was also the architect of the Teatro della Pergola" (Radcliffe, *op. cit.*, p. 22).

It is important to recognize, however, that despite the emphasis on the frontal presentation of the group, the bronze was conceived to accommodate numerous secondary vantage-points as well. The side and three-quarter views are complex and stimulating, and

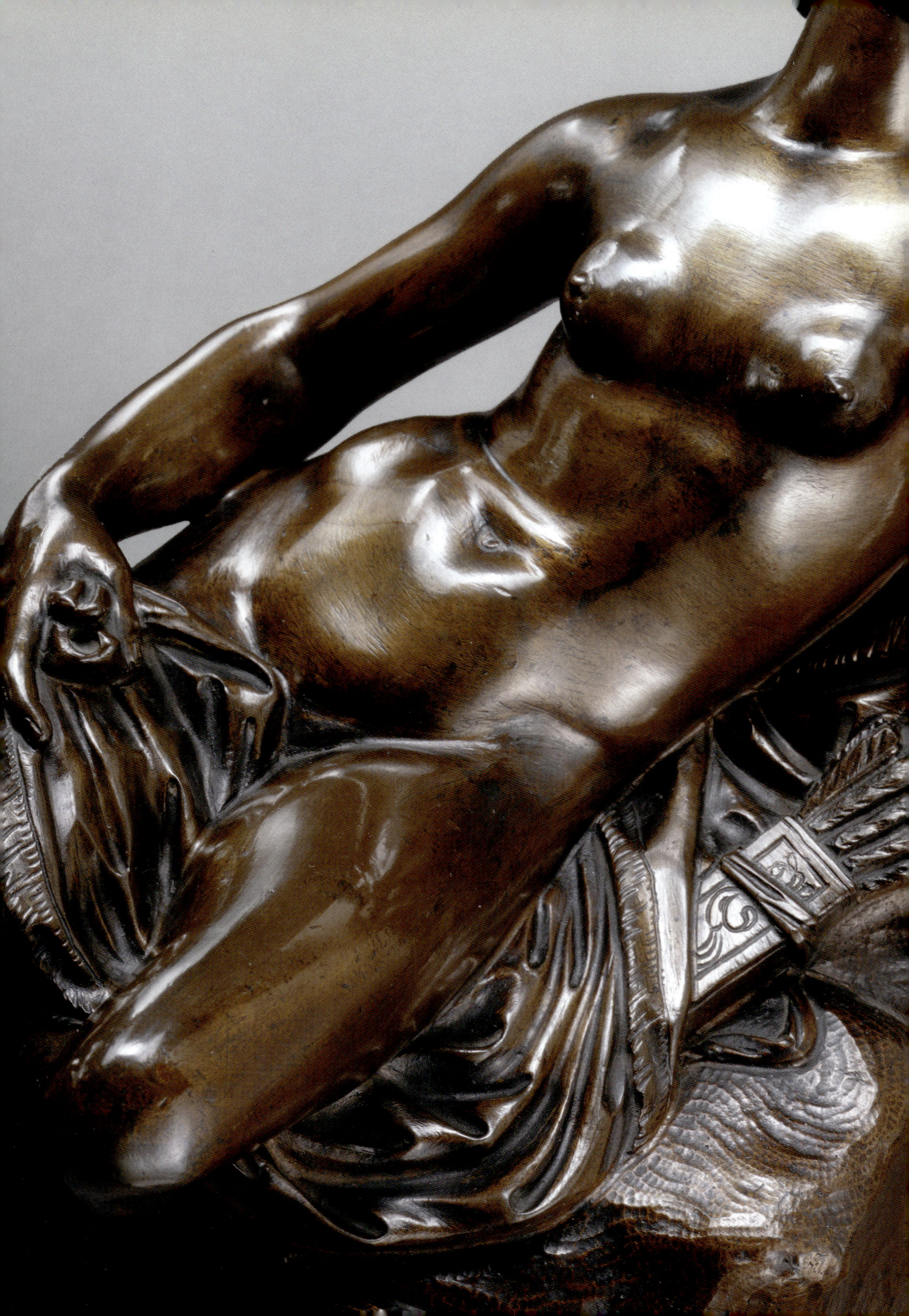

fig. 1 fig. 2

the back of the sculpture is of consummate beauty, and nearly equal in interest to the front view.

The finishing of the bronze is of exquisite precision. The punch-work and hammering of the ground and tree-trunk is highly detailed and is arranged in patterns of swirling intensity. Moreover, Ferdinando has taken great care in the chasing and polishing of the bronze to carefully distinguish between the character of the different materials represented. This is perhaps clearest in the back view of the sculpture; note, for example, how the ground, and the hair, skin, and cloak of Diana are each given a distinct appearance of texture. Chasing of this kind is of the highest level of quality, rivaling anything in the Giambologna tradition. The rich, reddish gold patina, too, is comparable to the best examples in Giambologna's statuettes.

This competition with the Giambologna tradition was fully intentional. Indeed, in this group Ferdinando Tacca clearly sought to reinterpret a well-known type of the older master. Perhaps as early as 1577, Giambologna had first made a bronze statuette depicting a sleeping nymph and satyr; one example of this type is illustrated in fig. 2. This proved to be an immensely popular composition, and variants were produced by Antonio and Gianfrancesco Susini as well as by Pietro Tacca, Ferdinando's father. Ferdinando's was the freest and most successful adaptation of the composition. As Charles Avery has commented:

"More interesting is the subtle 'melting down' of the forms. . . by Ferdinando Tacca. . . . By the introduction of the conveniently shaped landscape base and a freer play in the figures Ferdinando succeeded at last in endowing Giambologna's heterogeneous group with a more satisfying feeling of unity and harmony" (Avery, 2000, *op. cit.*, pp. 53–54).

Andrew Butterfield

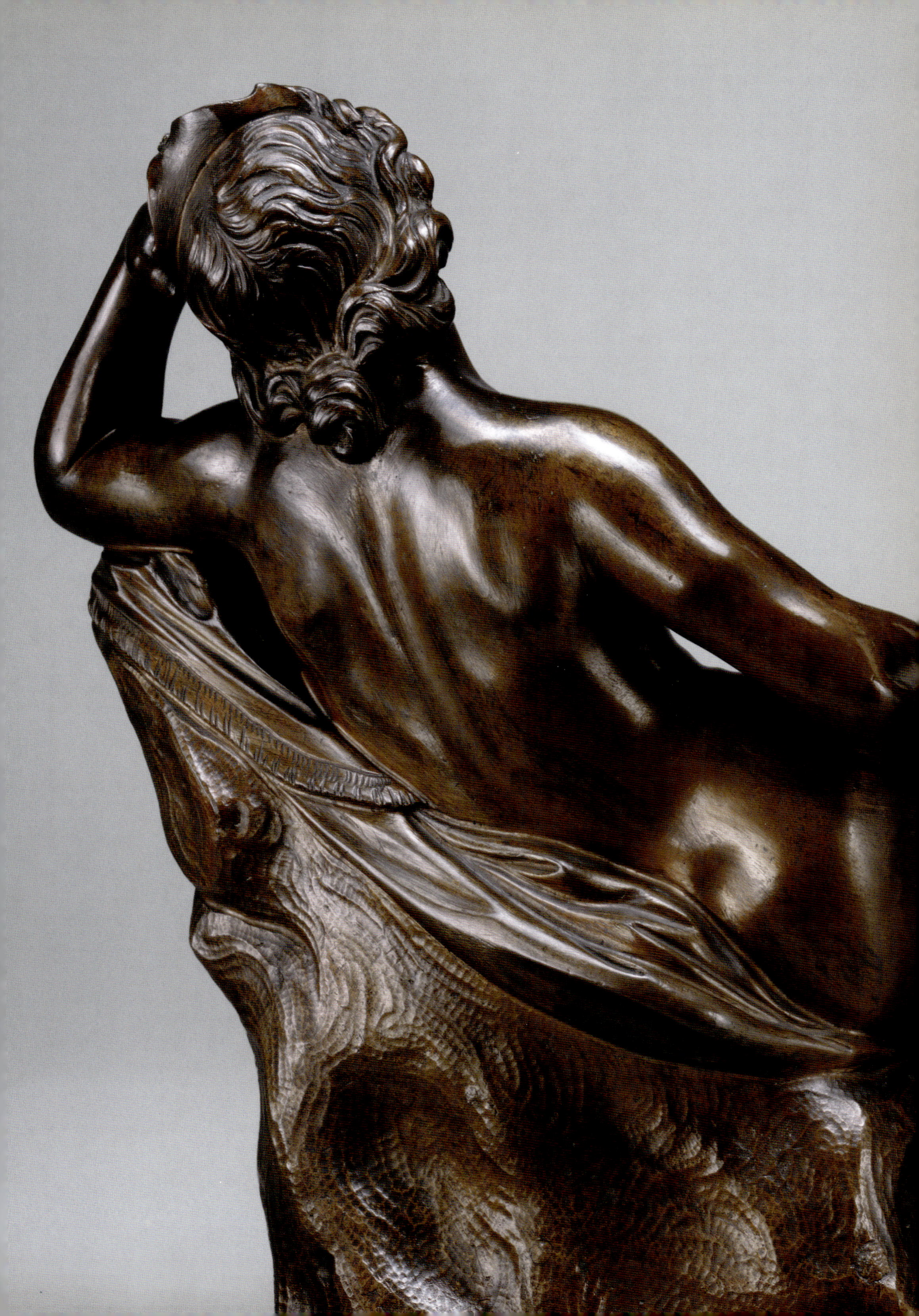

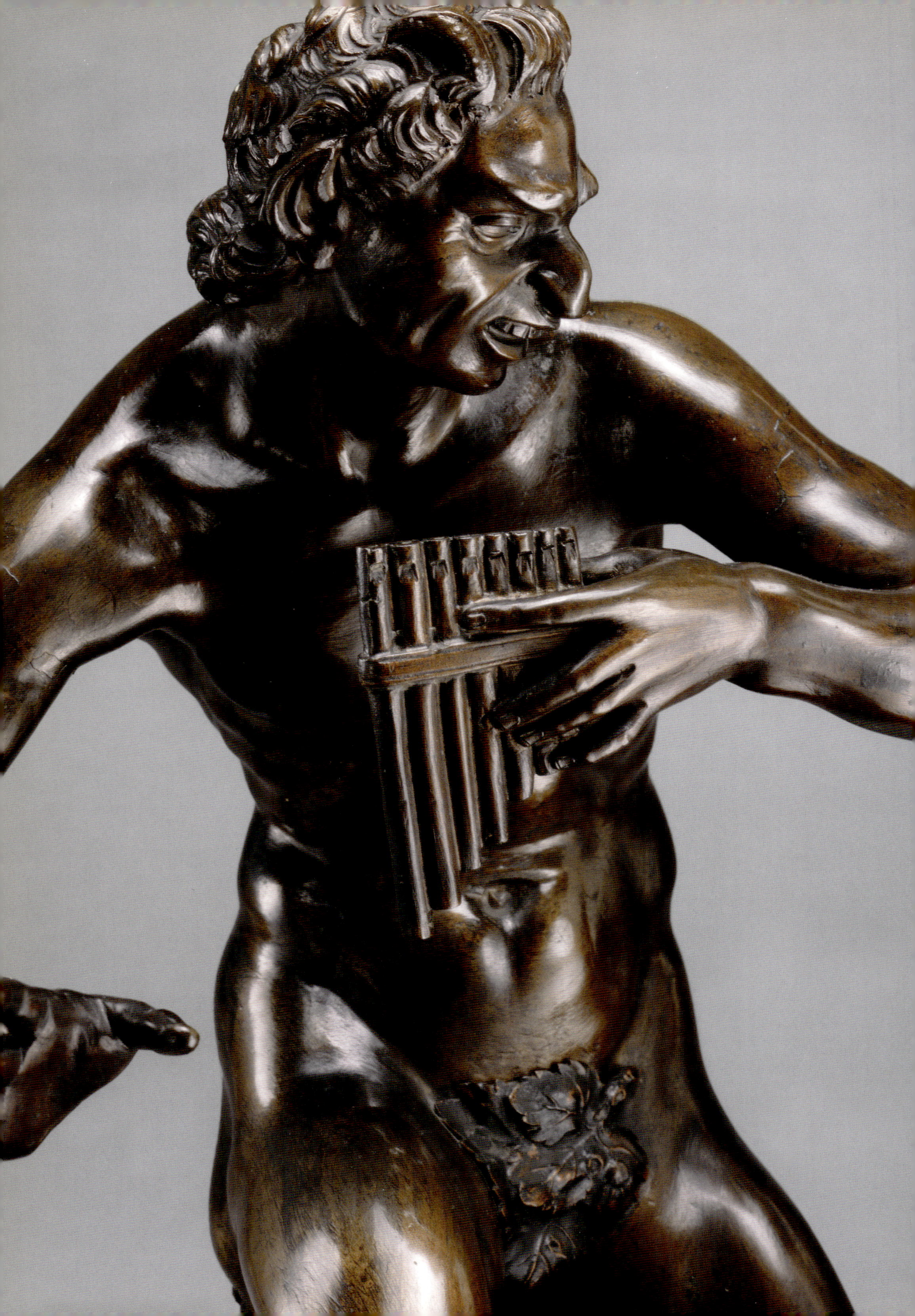

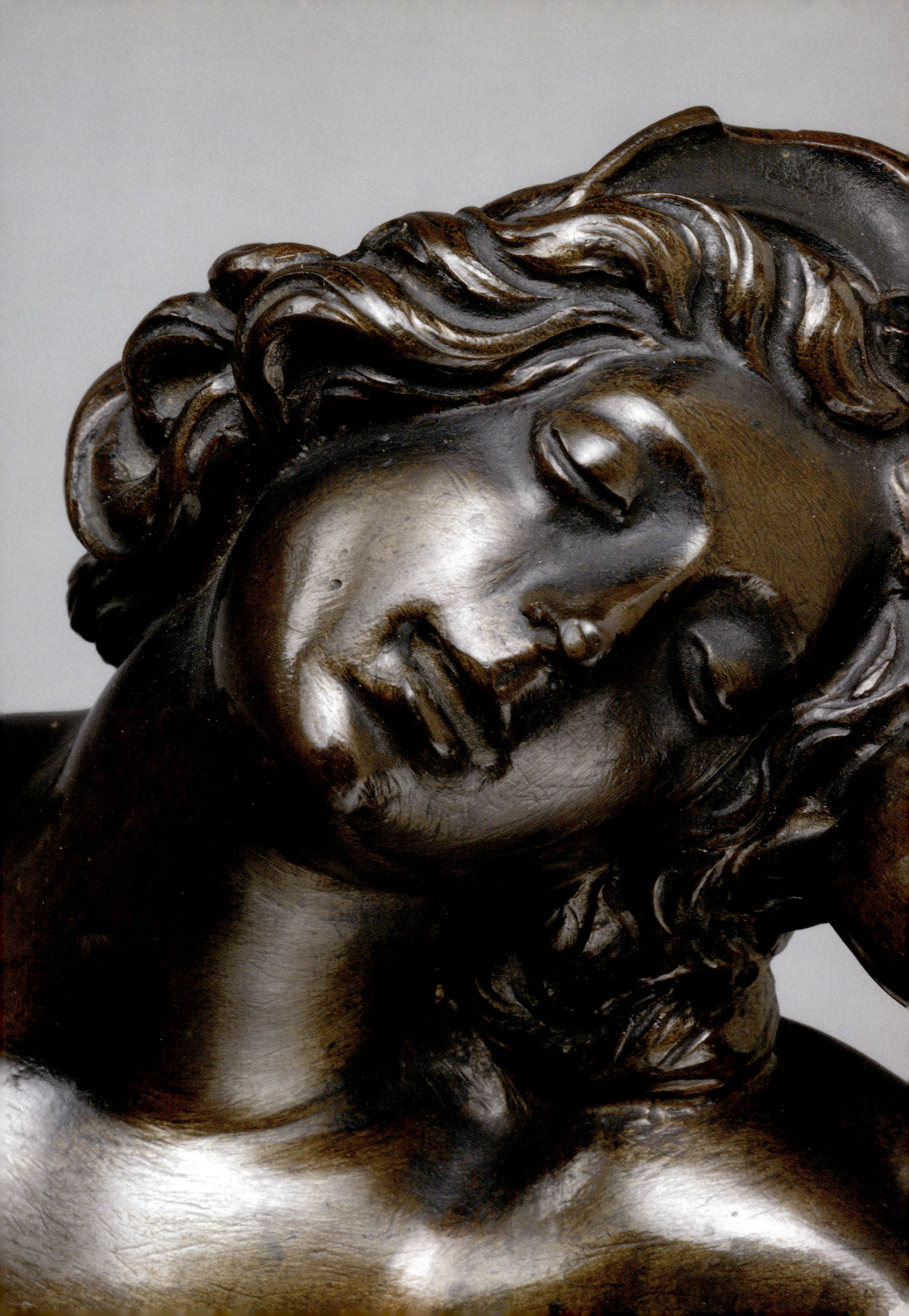

GIAN LORENZO BERNINI
(Naples 1598–Rome 1680)

Portrait of a Gentleman

Marble
54.5 cm. (21⁷⁄₁₆ in.) high
c. 1670

Provenance:

Antonio Munoz, Rome
Antonia Nava-Cellini and Pico Cellini, Rome
Taddei Family Collection, Lugano,
Giancarlo Gallino, Turin
Private Collection, Europe

Bibliography:

U. Schlegel, "Gian Lorenzo Bernini: Ritratto di Pietro Bernini," in *Per la storia della scultura. Materiali inediti e poco noti*, ed. by M. Ferretti, Turin, 1993, pp. 103–109

C. Avery, *Bernini: Genius of the Baroque*, Boston, New York, Toronto, London, 1997, p. 14, fig. 8 (illustration is reversed)

S. Bruno, in *Gian Lorenzo Bernini: Regista del Barocco* (exh. cat. Palazzo Venezia, Rome, 21 May–16 September 1999), Milan, 1999, p. 311, no. 24

A. Sigel, "The Technical Study of a Terracotta Modello of *The Moor*," in *Bernini: the Modello for the Fountain of the Moor* (exh. cat. Salander-O'Reilly Galleries, New York, 4 December 2002–1 February 2003), New York, 2002, p. 68

See separate catalogue.

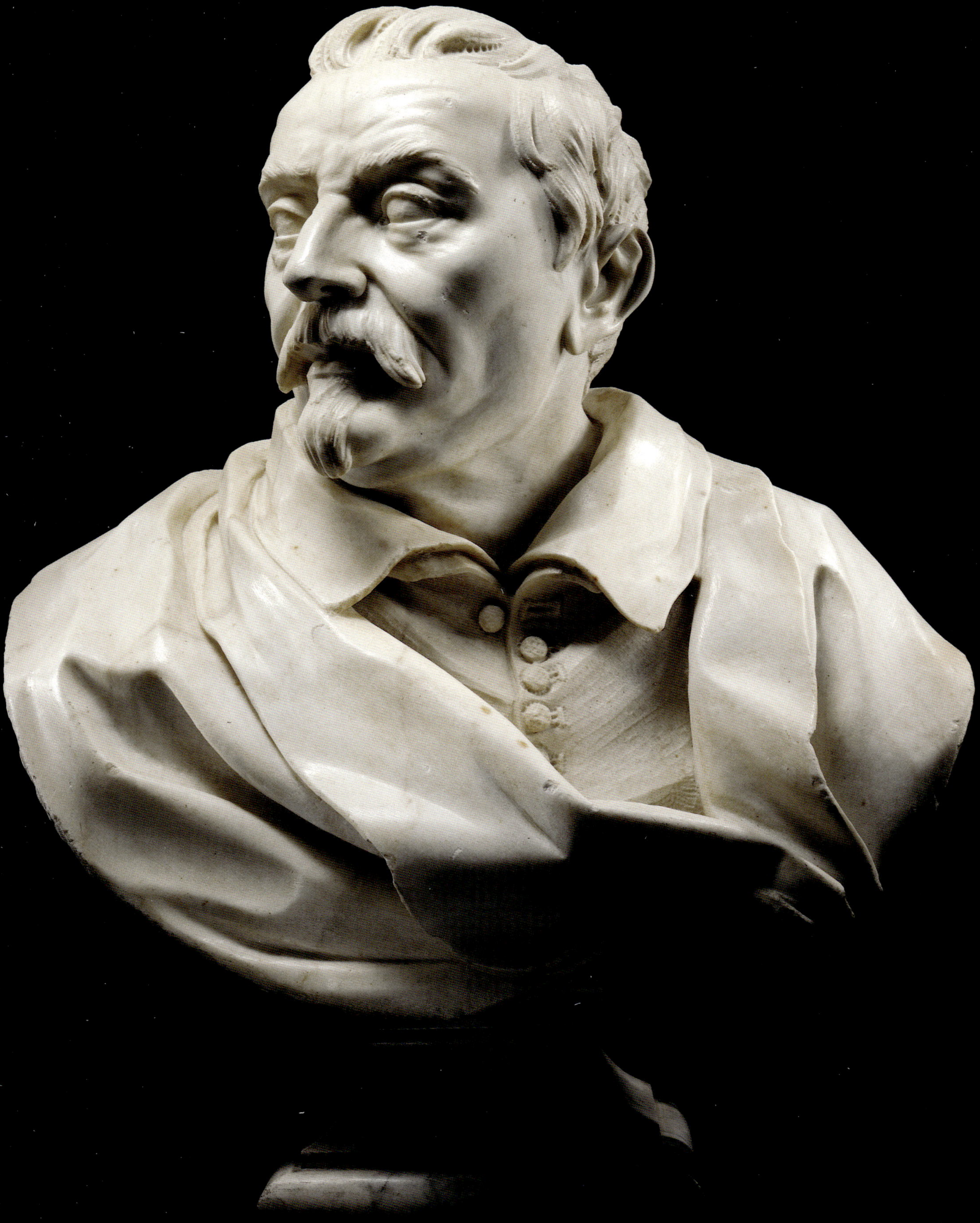

Contributors

Andrew Butterfield is Senior Vice-President of Salander-O'Reilly Galleries and the author of more than sixty articles and books, including *The Collection of Victor and Sally Ganz*, *The Jacques Koerfer Collection*, *Early Renaissance Reliefs*, and *The Sculptures of Andrea del Verrocchio* for which he won the Eric Mitchell Prize.

Francesco Caglioti is Professor of Art History at the University of Naples and the author of *Donatello e i Medici: storia del David e della Giuditta* (Florence, 2000) and many other publications on Italian Renaissance sculpture and painting, particularly in Tuscany, Rome, Naples and South Italy.

Giancarlo Gentilini is Professor of Art History at the University of Perugia. His publications include *I Della Robbia. La scultura invetriata nel Rinascimento*, and *I Della Robbia e l' "arte nuova" della scultura invetriata*.

Gert Kreytenberg is Professor of Art History at the Kunstgeschichtliches Institut at Ruhr-Universität Bochum. His books on Italian Trecento sculpture include *Tino di Camaino*, *Andrea Pisano und die toskanische Skulptur des 14. Jahrhunderts*, and *Orcagna, Andrea di Cione: ein universeller Künstler der Gotik in Florenz*.

Jeanette Sisk received her Master of Arts degree from the Institute of Fine Arts at New York University and is a research associate at Salander-O'Reilly Galleries.

In most cases the comparative illustrations have been made from photographs and transparencies provided by the owners or custodians of the works. Those figures for which further credit is due are listed below:

Giovanni Antonio Amadeo, *Pietà*: fig. 1 courtesy of Domenico Lucchetti

Girolamo Santacroce, *Saint John the Baptist* and *Saint Benedict*: fig. 3 courtesy of Luciano Pedicini

© 2004 Salander-O'Reilly
ISBN: 1-58821-129-0

Translations: Uwe Bergermann and
Antonia Reiner-Franklin
Color photography: Maggie Nimkin
Design: Lawrence Sunden, Inc.
Printing: Randem Printing Co.